House Beautiful

D0128263

The Organized Home

House Beautiful

The Organized Home

Stylish Storage
Solutions for
Every Room

By C. J. Petersen

HEARST BOOKS
A division of Sterling Publishing Co., Inc.

New York / London
www.sterlingpublishing.com

The Library of Congress has cataloged the hardcover edition as follows:

Petersen, C. J.
  House beautiful, designed to order : stylish solutions to organize your home / C.J. Petersen.
      p. cm.
  Includes bibliographical references and index.
  ISBN 1-58816-444-6 (alk. paper)
1. Storage in the home. 2. Interior decoration.
I. Title: Designed to order. II. House beautiful.
III. Title.
  TX309.P48 2006
  648'.8--dc22
2005013110

10 9 8 7 6 5 4 3 2 1

Book design by Alexandra Maldonado
Illustrations by Carol Ruzicka

Published by HEARST BOOKS
A Division of Sterling Publishing Co., Inc.
387 Park Avenue South,
New York, NY 10016

House Beautiful and Hearst Books are registered trademarks of Hearst Communications, Inc.

www.housebeautiful.com

For information about custom editions, special sales, premium and corporate purchases, please contact Sterling Special Sales Department at 800-805-5489 or specialsales@sterlingpublishing.com.

Distributed in Canada by
Sterling Publishing
c/o Canadian Manda Group
165 Dufferin Street
Toronto, Ontario, Canada M6K 3H6

Distributed in Australia by
Capricorn Link (Australia) Pty. Ltd.
P.O. Box 704
Windsor, NSW2756 Australia

Printed in China

Sterling ISBN 13: 978-1-58816-682-1
       ISBN 10: 1-58816-682-1

TABLE OF CONTENTS

foreword

The homes pictured in the pages of House Beautiful are all shown at their best, but make no mistake, those homes are just like yours when it comes to the continual battle against clutter. It makes no difference whether your home is old or new, big or small or decorated in a modern or period style, clutter seems to sneak in no matter what. It's a hard problem to defeat precisely because it's so difficult to even identify. If you're like me, when you spend ten or fifteen minutes looking for your keys, you curse your memory. You don't stop to realize you really have no set place to put your keys every time you walk in the door. Maybe you've felt the frustration of moving a pile of backpacks and jackets from kitchen table to chair just so you can serve dinner. Well, take heart—you're far from alone. Most of us find that keeping our homes organized is a continual struggle.

When you get right to the heart of it, clutter is a design issue. Not only does it detract from your home's aesthetic, it is itself a symptom of poor design. You can have all the frantic spring-cleaning days you want, but if your home isn't designed with a common-sense place for everything you own, you'll always have a clutter problem. Thoughtful, attractive, use-oriented design is at the foundation of any well-planned home. A functional design philosophy guides you toward design elements that are both pleasing to look at and helpful in organizing your space.

Approaching your kitchen with this philosophy means you have to make some small changes to your home's design to accommodate the inevitable trail of gear, clothing and other materials created by families. The solution lies in using vertical space: all those backpacks, jackets, sweaters and other loose items that clog surface areas are going to have a place to hang.

There will also be changes in other parts of the house to help keep the kitchen clear. For instance, by dedicating an antique basket in your entry hall to unopened mail, accumulating letters, catalogs and direct mail promotions won't find their way into the kitchen.

Logical solutions and strategies like these form the heart of this design philosophy, and you'll find a wealth of them in this book. It doesn't matter whether your particular organizational challenge lies in the bedroom, bathroom, or living room, because the author dissects each room in turn. Each chapter focuses on one room, leading you through assessing the sources of clutter, determining the fixes, and putting design changes in place. Along the way you'll find innovative storage solutions that complement your décor, regardless of what type of architecture and interior design you have. Universal clutter-beating rules begin each section, and more

than 200 images clearly illustrate how your home can be designed to encourage order. We've included style guides to help you sift through the many different options available to you, as well as tips and hints on how to adapt organization solutions in your own home. Clutter has been the bane of stylish home design for too long; now its banishment can be part of the beautiful picture that is your home at its best.

From the Editors of *House Beautiful*

introduction

Clutter is the enemy of any home design. It's not only unattractive, masking the underlying decorative elements that make your home beautiful, it also makes life difficult in a number of ways. The disorganization that breeds clutter costs you valuable time making you search for what should be apparent and causing immense frustration in the process. Clutter lessens how you enjoy your home because you continually feel as if things are out of place and untidy. You regularly clean and organize your home, but it's hard to solve the clutter problem on a permanent basis. Pick up a child's room and a week later you can't find the bed for clothes and toys. Straighten your desk and you have the satisfaction of a tidy workspace... until next month, when you're frantically looking for an important receipt under piles of unopened mail and unread catalogs.

The problem is we are creatures of habit. If there is an easy, apparent and logical place to put a jacket when we come in the door, we'll quickly get in the habit of hanging up the jacket. On the other hand, if there's no place to accommodate a jacket, we'll get in the habit of tossing it onto the closest piece of furniture.

That's why the ultimate solution to disorganization and clutter has to be built in, a part of the very design of our homes. This is the core principle behind *The Organized Home*—a philosophy that will help you organize your home as you improve your décor.

Clutter doesn't happen by accident. It's the result of not having a proper place to put things. It's that simple. In some cases, it's a matter of getting rid of the item itself—its "place" is with a local charity, in a garage sale or in the garbage. But in most cases, you need to give all the clutter of your house—loose clothes, magazines, kitchen utensils—a clearly defined place to go. And it's best if this place is itself a design element, for instance a set of stylish hooks by the front door or a sleek hanging rack in the kitchen. When organization is part of the design of your house, it becomes second nature in your life. An interior design that actually helps you avoid disorder is naturally streamlined, resulting in both visual appeal and efficiency.

The wonderful part of this functional aesthetic philosophy is that it's not hard to put in place. In fact, it's all about ease—easy design solutions that are easy to maintain and easy to enjoy. It's just a matter of thinking through your clutter challenges and designing common-sense solutions. This book will lead you through that process room by room.

You'll also find the basic concepts extremely adaptable. For instance, the book illustrates how hanging things up can be an effective organizational technique in the kitchen, but you can use the same principle in other rooms, or adapt your own types of hanging storage to the kitchen. Although you can find a wealth of organizational systems and accessories in stores, you should always keep an open mind to devising your own solutions, which will give your home a signature look. Why spend money on a drawer organizer when that vintage lunchbox you love can add flair and provide the necessary storage for your napkins and napkin rings?

The best way to put this philosophy—and this book—into practice is to begin with your messiest room. There is usually one room in any house that seems to attract disorder and chaos. It might be the central gathering place,

such as an eat-in kitchen, or the point of entry where everything gets dropped, such as a large foyer. Wherever it is, your own clutter trouble spot is the place to start. Find the chapter dedicated to that room and begin with the boxed guidelines near the beginning of each chapter. These are principles that can guide and inform your decisions. Although they are most applicable to the room with which they are linked, these are general guidelines that often apply to other rooms in the house as well. A principle that brings order to the bedroom may be just as effective in keeping the family room tidy.

Each chapter outlines the basic elements of organization for a given room, and leads you through potential choices you can make based on the style of your home and your own needs and tastes. Remember that the chapters work together: the answer to disorder in one room may lie with a change to another room. That avalanche of magazines covering your coffee table may be best organized in racks in your home office. So while you're proceeding room by room, remain flexible and the solutions will often present themselves.

Throughout the book, we've included tips and hints that will make organizing that much easier. You'll also find stunning photos that illustrate effective clutter-beating strategies, and illustrated sections that show multiple ways to solve your organizational challenges. So turn the page and take your first steps toward stylishly designing clutter out of your home forever.

the composed bedroom

Making Room for Sleep and Romance

a restful refuge

Bedrooms are sanctuaries where we find renewal in sleep and a cozy place to indulge in intimacy. Disorder in this intensely personal space can disrupt our lives in ways small and large—from restless sleep to frustrating searches for your favorite shirt. The key to keeping your bedroom stylishly organized is to break with convention. The usual formula of bed table, bed, dresser and clothes closet is often ineffective in stopping the disarray that can be so jarring in the bedroom. A nightstand without a real purpose can become just another potentially cluttered surface; you would be better off without it. A closet with no rhyme or reason as to how clothes are stored only leads to clothes clutter everywhere else. It might make sense to reorganize the closet and use additional shelving to store clothes elsewhere in the room. Whatever your particular solutions, they must efficiently facilitate the two basic purposes of the bedroom: rest and romance.

▶ Clear Separation The well-defined sitting area in this bedroom creates a place to read before bed. Although the bed has a reading lamp, the absence of bed tables ensures papers and books don't migrate from the reading area. The shelves display a collection of antique jars and chests, discouraging their use as resting places for odds and ends.

Simple Design: Because the bedroom usually isn't subjected to the traffic problems common to other rooms such as kitchens and living rooms, clothes and what you do with them pose the single biggest challenge in a bedroom. Well-designed closet space is one part of the answer, but there are other ways to organize and store your clothes that can allow you to exercise decorative creativity.

Because the bedroom requires less furnishings than other rooms, a few informed choices in picking the right furniture for the way you live will also go a long way toward keeping the space free from the pandemonium of clutter.

Just as important as the furnishings you include are those you leave out. For instance, as severe as it may sound, a TV doesn't belong in a well-ordered bedroom. The TV brings with it remote controls, DVDs, videotapes and other mess-producing items that counter the two main purposes of the room. Piles of magazines or unread books are equally disruptive. You usually read one book or magazine at a time, so that's exactly how many

◀ Small Order In a tiny bedroom it is crucially important to limit surface space to prevent clutter that can quickly overrun the room. Here, a stack of books is used as a nightstand, and a small antique cabinet leaves just enough room for a vase. The reading lamp clips to the modest iron bed frame, taking up as little space as possible.

1 Maximize Closets: Getting your closets in order is the first step toward keeping clothes under control and making dressing a pleasure rather than a chore.

2 Dress Your Décor: Clothing, towels, bed linens and sartorial accessories can all be used as interesting graphic elements. Store attractive colorful garments in the open where they not only serve as design features, they'll also be more accessible.

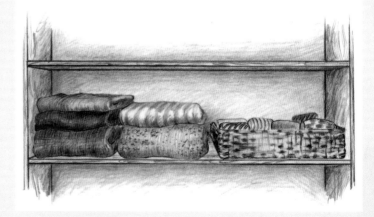

3 Stash for the Seasons: Seasonal items, from guest bed linens to winter clothes, need to be rotated in and out of long-term storage. Integrate handsome hideaways for these items rather than just stuffing them in any available space.

4 Furnish for Use: Choose bedroom furniture that explicitly serves your needs without wasted surface or drawer space and you'll be taking a big step toward keeping your bedroom clutter-free.

should be kept next to your bed. Exercise bikes are popular additions to the bedroom, but if you include one be sure to keep clothes off it and in the closet, where they belong. Let your furniture reinforce function and the bedroom will become the calm haven it's meant to be.

closet couture

Lack of closet space is an almost universal complaint, but more often than not the real problem is a matter of how the existing space is used. First and foremost, closet configuration needs to make sense. If most of your clothing is stored on hangers, you may need to eliminate shelves to accommodate extra hanging rods. If your shoes are out of control, you need dedicated shelves or other organizers where they can be lined up in an orderly display. Closet storage also needs to be somewhat adaptable, changing with the seasons and as you discard old clothing or buy new (or as the number of people using the bedroom changes). Consequently, the best closet systems are flexible in design, allowing you to periodically alter what is stored where. Finding or building the right closet system for you and your clothing is essential; a disorganized closet not only makes clothing hard to find, garments that should be in the closet will inevitably find their way out into other areas of the bedroom.

Variety of Choices: Whether you're modifying existing closet space or have decided to completely renovate the closet, you'll find a fantastic range of closet systems and accessories in retail stores. You can choose from large, adjustable systems that let you configure hanging poles, drawers, and shelves as you wish, or pick out individual elements—such as tie racks, belt hangers, or shoe holders—that suit your particular needs. You can also opt to build a custom unit to your precise specifications.

shop smart

There's never been a wider assortment of storage boxes designed to be both functional and beautiful. Choose from wood, fabric, or metal boxes in every color of the rainbow. When you need to see inside, don't feel confined to translucent plastic boxes; you can select from woven fabric and open-weave boxes that allow you to see in with style. Make a color scheme in or out of the closet with a grouping of boxes in different shades of the same color family. Regardless of your choice, measure first to make sure you get boxes that will be as useful as they are pleasing to the eye.

orderly innovation

Parents—especially those with small children—regularly use the bedroom as a place for the whole family to gather and relax. If your bedroom is sometimes used as a family room, simply accommodate the space to this additional use. Make sure you keep plenty of extra pillows on hand so that everyone can comfortably lounge, and keep a secondary toy box in your room (in a chest that fits the décor) so that children know that even in your bedroom toys need to be put away when they aren't being used. Make an area in nightstand drawers for pads of paper and crayons or pencils so that the kids can draw and write, and keep moist towelettes in the dresser or nightstand to clean up any food or beverage spills.

▲ **Styled Storage** Sweaters folded and stacked as they would be in a retail store, and coordinated by color, work with colored hangers to make this closet a truly attractive composition. A door seems almost unnecessary.

As with the rest of the bedroom, look beyond the conventional. Although some articles of clothing must be hung up to preclude being ruined, most of your clothes can just as easily be folded carefully and placed on a shelf. Shelves are generally more efficient than clothes hangers, because folded clothes take up less space. Sweaters and other knits are also less likely to get stretched out.

In addition to basic flat shelves, you can select from a variety of specialized shelving, such as "cubbyhole" shelving that has slots for shoes. Solid shelving is generally the best and most attractive choice for bedroom storage. Wire shelving provides an unsuitable surface for clothes and other soft goods, leaving impressions on fabric and letting loose items fall through. The exception is wire shoe racks.

Closet drawers can be a convenient way to store items such as cuff links, stockings and ties that always seem to clutter up the drawers in a dresser. Glass-fronted drawers let you quickly see what's inside and can add a touch of elegance to the closet. Avoid deep drawers except for pillows or blankets. They can increase confusion and clutter as you dig through trying to find something. The type of closet storage you choose is ultimately going to depend upon the

◀ **Top Hat** This walk-in closet could just as easily be a pleasing open display. Everything is placed for quick and easy access, with cubbyhole shelves to hold folded shirts and sweaters, hooks for hats, and long vertical hanging space for dresses and overcoats.

type and number of clothes you need to store. You'll find an analysis on pages 26 and 27.

Shoes: The jumble of shoes piled haphazardly in the bottom of closet—and often spilling out of it—is a chronic clutter problem in most bedrooms. But there are many ways to store shoes to keep them organized and accessible. Shoe shelves are a straightforward solution that is pleasing to the eye. Dedicated to footwear, these shelves are typically 12" deep and often canted so that the backs of the shoes sit higher than the fronts. Cubbyhole shelving can also be an ideal shoe-arranging system.

style file

Hooks have become more than utility items; the amazing variety of hanging implements available includes chrome, wrought iron, ceramic, clear resin, and other materials. Each type comes in a multitude of shapes, from a simple elbow to sweeping, elegant curves. Where you need several hooks, consider a hanging unit with a series of hooks on a wood or metal backing strip.

Sartorial Space-Saver

The well-dressed man needs a well-appointed closet, even when there isn't a lot of room to spare. This space holds a diverse and luxurious wardrobe, all organized in an efficient, logical fashion so that dressing is easy and a pleasure.

1 A wealth of shoes is kept neatly arranged on closely stacked shelves. The shoes have been arranged with dress shoes on top, casual shoes on the bottom. Even boots work on the shelves, with each pair arranged face-to-face.

2 Sweaters follow a seasonal and color breakdown. The brighter and lighter pieces are stacked at the bottom, and the darker and heavier garments are placed higher up.

3 A half-column of drawers provides a replacement for a dresser, organizing socks and underwear and helping keep dressing centralized.

4 The step stool is necessary to reach high shelves (including those not pictured) over the hanging clothes. Special-occasion scarves, ties, and other accessories are kept in attractive boxes stacked on the shelves.

5 A hook on the back of the door provides a place to put suits and jackets that have been pulled out for dressing.

SAVVY CLOSET CONFIGURATIONS

Sometimes you can have the wrong closet without knowing it. Designing the right closet configuration for your clothing and linens takes thought, so if you find your things are often in a jumble and you can never seem to find what you're looking for, it's time to assess just what type of space you need. Adapt the version that best suits your clothing and style.

Hanging Around Busy professionals tend to have a large number of formal or business garments, such as suits or dresses, which can't be folded. If your wardrobe consists of these "unfoldables," make sure you have all the hanging space possible. Giving your fine clothes extra space to hang free will keep them wrinkle-free and in good shape, and keep you looking great.

Long-Term, Short-Term If your home is short on hideaway storage space, you may need to arrange your bedroom closet to efficiently accommodate both everyday and long-term storage needs. The wisest move is to partition off the closet so that one section has room for hanging clothes, shelves close together for folded clothes, and an area just for shoes. The other part should have shelves spaced far apart to allow for large storage boxes and bins, and a small amount of long-term hanging space for seasonal clothing.

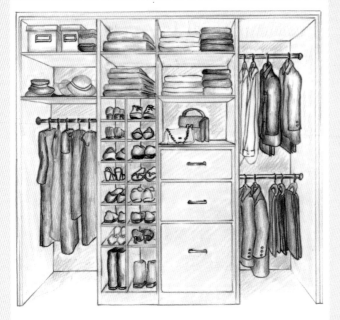

The Great Divide Sharing closet space can be a true test of a couple's relationship. The secret to keeping the peace is to divide the space in a way that accommodates the amount and type of clothing each person has. Women generally have a greater selection of hanging clothes and shoes. Men usually need more space for folded items such as short-sleeved shirts. Create a barrier between the two sections with a column of shelving and drawers or bins.

Shelf-Esteem Sometimes an informal wardrobe calls for an entirely different approach to closet organization. If all your clothes can easily be folded, it may make sense to eliminate hanging storage entirely, or at least limit it. Instead, use a mix of cubby and open shelving, drawers, and storage accessories such as hooks that better suit the simple nature of the clothes. The additional shelving gives you the flexibility to use other containers such as boxes, bins, and slide-out trays.

The only drawback is that you need to match the number of slots to the number of pairs of shoes you have, and the cubbyholes are not as effective for boot storage. For a less formal look, try hanging shoe pockets, which can be hung on a wall or concealed on the back of a closet door.

Hanging Clothes: Correctly estimating your needs is the trick to accommodating your hanging clothes properly. The safest way to ensure proper rod placement is to calculate the space you need before installing the rod. With the clothes on hangers, lay them flat on a surface and measure how high the pile is. Then add two inches per hanger and you have the length of hanging rod you need. A man's closet generally requires at least two hanging rods that can be placed one over the other, and possibly more if the man has a sizeable wardrobe of business suits. Keep in mind that, as a general rule of thumb, shirts, suits, and pants need 45 inches of vertical space to hang without interference.

A woman usually requires different hanging storage. Dresses call for a longer vertical space, which means that in addition to a rod allowing for 45 inches of space so that blouses can hang freely, there should be a rod placed 64 to 72 inches above the floor (depending on whether she has full-length dresses). Hanging clothes take up more room than you might think, because they should have enough space

▲ **Perfect Combo** An excellent blend of hanging storage and shelves provides ideal organization for this man's closet. Casual pants have been placed on the top hanging bar, while dress slacks are hung folded on the lower bar. Organizing by type makes the clothes easier to find, and folded pants take less vertical hanging space than unfolded ones.

between them to hang without touching. Cramming hanging clothes into the closet results in wrinkled clothing.

Folded Clothes: Folded clothing not only takes up less room than it would if it were hung up, it also presents an opportunity to create decorative accents. Group similar items together (e.g., sweaters with sweaters), arranged by colors, and place on shelves that are as close as possible to eye level, so you can locate everything at a glance.

Linens and Towels: Sheets, blankets, and towels all take up a lot of space. If possible, towels and washcloths should be taken out of the bedroom closet and stored closer to where they will be used. If not, put towels on a shelf with a lot of clearance to make moving the towels on and off the pile easier. If shelf

▼ Up Side The hanging bars in this woman's closet have been tucked in the end space, leaving lots of space for wall-mounted shelves and drawers. The drawers alleviate the need for a formal dresser. Notice that the floor is left clear and free of clutter.

style file

If you opt for a prefab closet system, you'll have a wide range of design styles from which to choose. On the low end, wire systems with pullout baskets and bins are inexpensive but unattractive. To make a closet stylish, choose from wood-veneered units available in dark and light finishes, or real wood that can be stained, given a natural finish, or painted whatever color suits your tastes. To add sophistication, include elegant finishing touches such as chrome shelf hardware, one or two glass shelves or frosted-glass drawer fronts.

space is at a premium in your closet, consider rolling towels tightly and storing them in a drawer or bin. This is a great technique that lets you grab a single towel quickly and easily when you need it. Bedclothes should be folded as neatly and compactly as possible and stored on a shelf or in a drawer.

Loose Accessories and Undergarments: For the most part, underwear, socks and other undergarments will most logically find a home in your dresser. But many closet organizing systems include drawers, which may eliminate the need for a separate dresser or allow you to use a smaller one. You can also opt for a more basic alternative by using colorful slide-out bins (either with rails that install underneath a shelf or those that just sit on a shelf) for socks, small garments, and accessories that don't need folding.

out of the closet

Bedroom storage options don't stop at the closet. Shelves, pegs, hooks, baskets, and chests are just some of the organizers that can help bring visually appealing order to the bedroom. You may want to consider removing as much as you can from the closet to ensure that it stays tidy and organized and to give you the maximum amount of room to maneuver in what is invariably a cramped space. Storing clothing out in the open also makes decorative elements out of your textiles while making them easier to retrieve.

Shelves and Ledges: A strategically placed shelf can supply the storage you need exactly where you need it. You can make a colorful, changeable display by arranging folded clothing on shelves in plain view. Consider stacking pastel sweaters grouped by color or arranging pants from gray to black. Getting

orderly innovation

Arranging clothing decoratively is as much art as science. Fortunately, there is plenty of free design advice available. Go to your favorite retail stores for inspiration, especially smaller boutiques, which must attractively display large quantities of clothing in close quarters.

▶ **Luxury Suite** The homeowner converted half of this large bedroom into a luxurious closet with plenty of room for clothes, accessories and a dressing area. The all-in-one nature of this walk-in closet ensures that clothes clutter doesn't find its way into the rest of the bedroom. The wealth of space allows for hanging garments to have plenty of separation and means that shelves don't have to be stuffed with clothes.

▲ **Plain View** Uncomplicated lines and a built-in bedside table accent this basic bedroom. A dresser can be eliminated in favor of shelves for a more orderly look. In addition, a series of rods can provide an attractive hanging storage for ties, scarves, belts, and other garments.

clothes out in the open also makes them easier to find when it comes time to put them on. Install narrower "ledge" shelves for smaller items like eyeglasses, cell phones, wallets and watches. For a nice touch that will keep loose items tidy, place a row of decorative bowls on a ledge and use them hold extra buttons, collar stays and similar items.

Hooks and Other Hangers: Hooks can be used for permanent display, as for a scarf collection, or for transitory items that move from one room to another such as towels. Create an interesting display with a row or grid of wood pegs holding hats, handbags, bathrobes, belts, necklaces, or other accessories.

Stand-alone Storage: Ties, belts, scarves, and other accessories can make for striking displays when arranged in their own unusual containers. For instance, an elegant serving tray can hold a display of rolled-up, multicolored ties arranged in rows. Nice towels and blankets can be brought out into the open, where they'll shine rolled up and positioned in a wicker basket or sticking out of clean, new, empty paint cans. Blankets are often appealing and are right at home folded neatly and placed on top of a cedar chest or rolled up to sit in a steel tub. Take the idea one step further by hanging colorful quilts from rods.

▲ **Covert Cargo** Shelves built into a nook surrounding the bed provide small, self-contained spaces that can be accessed only from the bed and therefore are less likely to collect general clutter. Underbed drawers provide long-term storage for linens and extra blankets.

finite furnishings

Furnishings in the bedroom should be few and hardworking. Aside from the bed, you'll probably have a dresser and nightstands. If you have the available space, you might include a small reading chair and lamp, but other pieces should be eliminated. The goal is to keep surface space to a minimum, because you're less likely to bring clutter into the bedroom if there is no place to put it.

Nightstands: When it comes to choosing nightstands, less is usually more. Although it seems as though drawers would be useful, in fact they are an invitation to store more junk then necessary near the bed. Medications should be kept in the bathroom, and most anything that would go in a bedside table is better kept elsewhere in the house. If you opt for drawers, organize whatever you keep in them, using plastic compartments, drawer dividers or organizers available at retail. Attempt to limit the size of the tables to the surface space you really need or clutter will fill in the extra space. Generally, you don't need much more than the area it takes to hold a lamp, a book and your alarm clock. Small, simple end tables are also more likely to complement a wide range of bedroom design styles. Don't limit yourself to what's for sale in stores—bed tables can be adapted from a range of sources, from wrought-iron plant stands to three-legged stools. You can even use a shelf or other wall-mounted structure positioned next to the bed as a nightstand. Start with your surface space needs, and then choose a material, color and overall look that fits in with your bed and other furniture.

Beds: The bed you choose is largely a matter of design preference, although beds can also provide storage as needed. Underbed drawers can be quite useful for storing seasonal clothes and large linens such as a comforter or blanket. The space under a standard bed frame can also provide a storage area for decorative boxes or plastic bins on wheels designed specifically for this purpose. Underbed storage should always be covered or self-contained (such as drawers built into a bed frame) to avoid dust.

Dressers: The dresser should suit the décor of the bedroom and should reflect the size of the space. An overly large dresser will crowd the bedroom and the top will attract an accumulation of objects that belong somewhere else. If you usually keep smaller items

◀ Shelf-ish Intentions Built-in shelves provide a neat and orderly place for books in the bedroom, as well as space for pictures. The shelves could just as easily serve as nesting places for colorful sweaters, linens, or stacks of folded pants.

such as cuff links in drawers, consider putting them in a decorative container on top of the dresser. That way, the top surface becomes a stage for decorative accents such as a raku or sterling silver bowl, and small items that so often become misplaced are easier to keep track of. Displaying items with purpose also takes up room that clutter might otherwise fill.

Chests: Storage chests for the bedroom come in all shapes and sizes. It's easy to adapt a chest to your needs. Just be sure to balance your storage needs against the rule of scale: the chest shouldn't dwarf the other pieces in the bedroom. Simple wood chests are widely available and can be painted, stained, stenciled, or finished to suit just about any design scheme. The right chest can provide ample storage and will serve as an accent piece that brings flavor to the room. From a steamer trunk to old luggage to a modern dark wood chest with clean and simple lines, this is your chance to add an outstanding focal point to your bedroom suite.

Wardrobes and Stand-alone Closets: Sometimes you simply have no closet space, in which case you have to create your own. Wardrobes come in a range of styles, from antique to contemporary. Measure for placement before shopping for a wardrobe, and then purchase based on the amount of clothing you need to conceal. Keep in mind that many clothes can simply be folded and placed on a shelf outside the wardrobe. If it seems like a wardrobe will overpower the space, a more functional solution may be a portable closet. These range from simple melamine boxes with hanging rods and wheels to metal frames on casters with a fabric shell. A portable closet gives you some flexibility in design, because you can customize the exterior.

◀ Side Dish A minimum of surface space is the hallmark of this simple and inviting bedroom. The designer has eliminated shelves, done without a chest at the foot of the bed, and used bed tables that provide just enough room for candles, a vase, and a small picture.

THE CASE FOR PORTABLE CLOSETS

A rolling closet is a great portable alternative to built-in storage. But a bare set of metal shelves or hanging rods on casters is too utilitarian for even the most spartan bedroom design scheme. A fabric closet case can dress up the unit to help it fit in with the rest of your furnishings. Choose a design and color scheme based on whether you want the closet to stand out as a focal point or blend in with your décor.

Flap Happy A basic flap in front pulls aside to reveal a hanging bar and bottom shelves to hold dresses and shoes in an attractive unit. A floral print is uncomplicated and will complement many different room décors.

Shady Storage Use a fabric case with a roman shade for a door to create an unconventional look. This striped case conceals hanging clothes used for long-term storage.

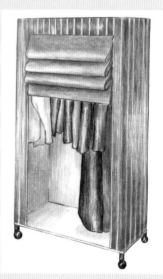

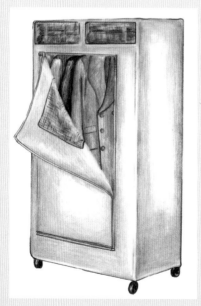

Room with a View Cut squares in the case and trim with piping to create windows revealing the folded clothes stored on the shelves. Add a sophisticated touch with sheer fabric panels attached from behind to cover the windows.

▲ **Double Duty** A single antique stand
serves as nightstand for two beds, with
a drawer to hold books or magazines for
bedtime reading and a small cabinet for
seasonal blankets.

◄ **Treasure Chest** This small, ornate chest adds a touch of the unusual to this bedroom and also provides a tidy storage place for extra bed linens or pillows.

the coordinated kitchen

Efficient Cooking and
Easy Socializing

new roles,
new organization

The kitchen has increasingly become the social center of the house, where families gather, friends snack and chat, and homeowners entertain. Given its many roles, it's no surprise that the kitchen has also become a magnet for clutter. Whether it's coats, scarves, pocketbooks and backpacks or unopened mail, unused appliances and superfluous gadgets, kitchen clutter can quickly accumulate. The problem is that so much of what clutters the kitchen seems like it belongs there. Seldom-used appliances, duplicated utensils, and the odds and ends that have migrated from other rooms all seem right at home, even as they help create a sense of chaos.

▼ **Round About** A lazy Susan allows this table to do double duty, providing a place for condiments and cooked foods when the table is used for eating and easy access to ingredients when it is being used as a preparation area.

▶ **Holding Cell** Oversized bowls are portable organizers for all kinds of foodstuffs, from vegetables to candy to fruit, and are temporary way stations for food during preparation. And they look fantastic no matter what they're holding.

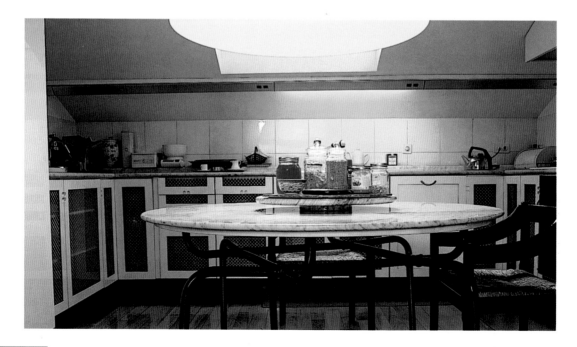

Focus on Functionality: The secret to bringing order to this high-traffic space involves utilitarian design elements. By designing around what you actually do in any given area of the kitchen, you reinforce good organizational habits. You're less likely to dump mail in an area that you've thoughtfully dedicated to food preparation, and utensils will be picked up more quickly if they have their own hooks or drawer slots awaiting their return.

The advantage you have in the kitchen is that the functions of different areas are well defined. You already know where you prepare food, wash dishes and clean up, cook, eat, and socialize. The design changes you make will simply emphasize the purposes of each of those areas.

The process is basic. First you'll weed out the things that don't belong at all. Next you'll determine the most logical locations for everything in the kitchen. Then you'll refine your kitchen's design, starting with the large structures and then moving to more modest organizational elements that make each area efficient and attractive. Along the way, you'll enhance the way your kitchen is used and the enjoyment you get out of it.

1 Locate by Function: Store items near where they will be used and they are less likely to become clutter. This also makes working in the kitchen that much easier.

2 Hide in Plain View: The great thing about the kitchen is that most everything in it, from food to utensils, has an inherent aesthetic appeal. Functional items can become a part of the design.

3 Hang It: Hanging hardware is amazingly stylish and adaptable and allows you to efficiently store frequently used equipment and supplies right where they'll be used. You can also incorporate unique hanging structures for a more personal touch.

4 Demand Double Duty: Bread baskets, water pitchers, and large mixing bowls are just some of the functional kitchen objects that can serve as stylish storage when not in use. Use them to create an impression of utilitarian panache.

Sleek Setting

This stylish, modern eat-in kitchen has many effective and fashionable organizational features.

1. Hanging rails in different work areas allow for utensils to be stored near where they are used most, and gives the cook a great deal of flexibility for items such as a cookbook holders.

2. The large amount of cabinetry— and the many variations in size of cabinets and drawers—ensures that there is a place for anything that needs to be stored in the kitchen.

3. Basic cabinets with frosted-glass fronts and interior lighting let everyone know just where to find dishes, cups and small appliances.

4. Countertop containers keep staples near at hand and augment the accessories storage found on the hanging rails.

5. A handy pull-out table can accommodate up to six diners. Pushed in, with a bowl as centerpiece, there is less open surface area to invite clutter.

6. Drawers on both sides of the island provide abundant storage and make it easier for several people to work in the kitchen at one time.

7. The finish of the island cabinets differentiates them from the general kitchen cabinets, visually indicating the fact that they are used for pantry items, while the rest of the cabinets house cookware.

▲ **Sleek Space** The simplest solution is best in this well-organized kitchen. A basic food preparation island serves as a focal point for cooking without becoming the obstacle to traffic flow that a large breakfast-bar island would have been.

start by streamlining

Bringing order to the kitchen begins with the process of clearing away what isn't used, isn't needed, and doesn't belong. Start with obvious duplications and items that have no purpose. Do you really need three wine-bottle openers or two can openers? Have you ever used those odd-shaped plastic containers you keep in the back of your cupboard? If the answer is no, toss them or give them away. Do the same with perishable, canned, and dried foods that have lounged too long on your shelf. As a general rule of thumb, if a box or can has been on the shelf more than a few months, you're probably not going to use it. So discard or donate it.

▼ **Clean and Green** This streamlined kitchen has been pared down to the essentials that fit neatly in the cabinets or on the simple shelves. The result is a clean and spare look with no clutter on the small workspace.

Maximize Free Space: There are also less obvious candidates for removal. These include any of the seemingly endless specialized utensils and appliances that fill today's cooking catalogs. It's easy to accumulate these kitchen "tools" with the idea of saving work on some specific culinary chore. But the hard truth is that there is no need to keep a mandoline you haven't used in years. Only when you've pared down to the utensils, gadgets, and supplies that you actually need will you know exactly what has to be organized.

Even though it's counterintuitive, consider freeing up space in the kitchen by relocating your cookbooks. The steam, odors, smoke, liquids, and other messes in a kitchen are unkind to books. Because you use only one at a time, cookbooks can be conveniently stored with the rest of your books. So keep them on a nice dry, clean bookshelf where they belong.

Finally, relocate anything that belongs in another room, from jackets to household tools to recycling bins that might better be kept in the garage. At the end of the process, there should be nothing left in your kitchen that doesn't have something to do with cooking, eating, or socializing over a meal. Or if you use the kitchen as a general room for other activities, such as doing homework, perusing catalogs, or playing board games, specific organization and storage solutions should be in place for those activities.

orderly innovation

Ledges are narrow shelves that provide specialized storage for areas in which a full-size shelf would be awkward or for smaller goods that can get lost on a bigger shelf. They keep the odds and ends of your kitchen from becoming clutter and prevent them from getting lost in a cabinet. For instance, a ledge can be a great undercabinet shelf for holding tiny spice jars or a row of demitasse cups.

▶ **Back to Basics** Custom-made cabinets in the kitchen are topped by marble counters and backsplashes. The antique French tin-topped cheese maker's table (in the foreground) adds a touch of the Old World. The focus is on function, but not at the sacrifice of a compelling aesthetic.

furniture and flow

Kitchen furnishings play a key role in determining how easy the kitchen is to use and how well organized it will be, not to mention setting the style of the space. Whether you're starting from scratch with a full renovation or are looking to make modest changes to your existing layout, your furniture choices should be guided by a commitment to practicality. The right furniture will actually help break the clutter habit, because you'll have the correct amount of storage space in the right locations for all your equipment, cookware, and dry goods. Consider each type of furniture separately to build a handsome combination of storage and organization solutions perfectly suited to your needs and the look of your kitchen.

Cabinetry: Cabinet space is often the most valuable real estate in the kitchen. Whether you're putting in new cabinets or working with existing units, try to optimize the space by creating specified storage areas. For instance, decide which cabinet will hold the canned goods, and then make sure you have the right cabinet capacity and that the shelves are adjusted properly to allow placement of and access to the range of canned goods you'll store. Organize your shelves as a shopkeeper would by placing multiples of the same product one behind the other with the labels facing out. If you decide to keep glasses and dishes in a cabinet, allow room around stacks and rows to prevent breakage. When choosing cabinets, opt for adjustable shelves to allow maximum flexibility in what will be stored where.

- **Specialty cabinets** can be wonderfully innovative solutions to common kitchen storage problems. No place to hang pots and pans? Replace undercounter cabinets with large pullout trays. No room for a pantry? Install a slide-out pantry system in existing floor-to-ceiling cabinet space. The possibilities are vast and begin with your needs. Look at what you need to store and then shop for the cabinet variation that best suits your kitchen.

- **Overcabinet storage** is a frequently overlooked asset yet can offer a more effective type of organization than using cabinets that run to the ceiling. If your ceilings are high, plan to use the space between the cabinet and ceiling. This will give the kitchen an open feeling and provide accessible storage. This area can serve as a place to keep appliances, baskets, and large serving platters and bowls in plain view so that finding them will be as simple as looking up. Ideally, you should reserve this area for less frequently used items. Keep a stepstool on hand so that every person in the house will be able to reach the area.

- **Glass fronts** are a great cabinet organization aid, and you should consider them for at least some of your cabinets. With a clean and elegant appearance, glass-fronted cabinets let you display your stemware and dishes in an attractive, orderly fashion, and allow other people to easily find items they need, even if they are not familiar with the kitchen. Glass-fronted cabinets are best fitted with interior lighting, both for a dramatic appearance and to make dishes easy to locate in a darkened kitchen. And because the contents are always in view, you'll be inclined to keep them neat.

- **Overall cabinet** layout is your chance to get creative with storage and organization. Although cabinets should be positioned where you need concealed storage, installing a run of identical cabinets above all available counter space may not be the best strategy. Instead, vary the position and number of cabinets to customize storage for specific work areas. It may make sense to leave wall space for built-in dish drainers, wine racks, customized hanging bars, or specialized caddies for bottles or flatware. Freestanding cabinets allow you to add accents to the kitchen décor and put storage space exactly where you need it. For instance, a freestanding pine cabinet might be ideal accessory storage for your country kitchen, providing a place to keep board games that are played at the kitchen table.

◀ **Country Clutter Killer** This rugged hutch not only provides a hallmark centerpiece for a country kitchen, it also offers abundant exposed shelving to show off an assortment of plates, glasses, cups, and crockery. The space below conceals less attractive items. If you have the room, a large stylish piece like this will let you organize a majority of kitchen items in one place.

orderly innovation

▲ **Pull Party** These stunning kitchen units include oversized pull drawers that can contain big items such as a large bag of potatoes or a turkey roasting pan.

◀ **Sleek and Brown** A variety of cabinet types help define this clutter-free kitchen. Special curved-front undercounter cabinets provide abundant storage for the island, while a pair of simple glass fronts provides an accent to the sleek, frameless cabinets.

You'll find a variety of drawer organizers on the market that can turn any drawer into a container dedicated to utensils, spices, bar implements, cutlery, and more. If your drawers tend to hold chaotic collections of disparate items, use prefab organizers to bring structure to the mess.

Shelving: Open shelving is in vogue as a viable substitute for cabinets. You can change the look of your kitchen and make stored items more accessible by replacing outdated cabinets with sturdy shelves. For a simple, fresh, and inexpensive alteration, take the doors off frameless cabinets and refinish the shells as built-in shelving units. Shelves can be an organizational boon because they force you to arrange dry goods and cookware in pleasing graphic patterns. This not only serves an aesthetic purpose, it also lets you see inventory at a glance.

Even in a traditional kitchen with standard top-and-bottom cabinetry, shelves provide added storage that can be reconfigured as needed or as the design of the kitchen changes. Modern stainless-steel shelving comes in freestanding units or single shelves, and the look complements an array of décors. Simple wood shelves can be painted any color to blend right in with walls or to contrast with the wall color and serve as a focal point. Assess your shelving needs based on what you can't or don't want to put in available cabinets. Just keep in mind that any items that can be hung

▲ **Open House** Simple floor-to-ceiling shelves provide easy access to dishes, placemats, and other kitchen necessities. Loose items are kept in wicker baskets, which add texture and visual interest while keeping order.

shouldn't sit on a shelf or in a cabinet. And as with cabinets, the best shelves are adjustable.

• **Freestanding shelves** can be moved around to accommodate changing kitchen design but can also be space hogs. Use freestanding units where you have significant open space. Measure carefully to ensure that the shelving unit not only fits into the kitchen layout but also allows plenty of room in front for traffic flow. You should have a clear idea of what will go on the shelving before you buy it, to avoid empty shelf space that will invite clutter.

◀ **Transparent Beauty** Glass-front cabinets provide great incentives for forcing yourself—and your family—to be organized. Any clutter or dishware put back in the wrong place will be all too apparent. In the kitchen at left, everyday dinnerware is neatly stored above the work surface, while the clutter of pots and pans goes beneath it.

- **Built-in shelving** can fit seamlessly into existing kitchen design. Built-in units should be as simple and unadorned as possible, so that they are easy to clean. These are an excellent choice for spaces you would otherwise dedicate to cabinets. They are also ideal for pantries, where accessibility is a paramount concern.

▼ **Sans Cabinets** A clean, rectangular wall-mounted box shelf provides a sleek alternative to cabinets, while abundant drawers in a breakfast bar/island offer copious hideaway storage for items too large for the shelf.

- **Wire shelves,** such as perennially popular restaurant shelving, are good choices for storing wide or flat objects, such as mixing bowls and dishes. The shelves themselves complement other steel accents and coordinate with just about any kitchen style. However, tall, thin bottles and top-heavy items such as wine glasses will tip over on wire shelves. Solid shelving provides better storage for stemware and similar shapes. Coated wire shelves are not only less attractive, they are awkward to clean, making wrought iron or stainless steel the preferred choices for a kitchen.

style guide

Shelving is as much a design element as it is storage. Solid shelving offers a wealth of surface appearances; you can select from colors, stains, natural wood grain, or stainless-steel finishes. Shelf supports and brackets also add to kitchen fashion. For instance, a sleek, modern kitchen calls for hidden supports, but a country kitchen can benefit from antique wrought-iron brackets. Simple painted and polyurethaned wood brackets can provide subtle accents to a contemporary kitchen.

Perfect Positioning

Accessibility is key to good organization; when something is easy to get at, it's easy to put back as well. To make for a comfortable and efficient kitchen— and one that looks stylish—make sure that whatever you use most is placed closest to work areas.

1. A rugged pot hanger has been crafted of nickel-plated plumbing pipe and connectors. The combination of oversized S hooks and ring-and-arm hangers ensures that all types of pots and pans can be hung. The hangers can be moved so that the arrangement can be adjusted to suit the cook.

2. Glass-front cabinets provide eye-pleasing storage for daily dishes. Items with less aesthetic value are kept in solid-front cabinets and drawers.

3. The kitchen has been designed with shelves built into a far wall, providing an area for little-used items such as cookbooks and decorative serving plates. The pretty plates add an attractive element to the kitchen while staying out of the main bustle and mess.

- **Solid shelving** is ideal for lighter items and in situations where the shelves need to match the color or grain of existing kitchen furnishings. Look for "keyhole" or other concealed mounting systems, because this type of floating shelf eliminates the need for brackets that can block access and collect dirt and spills.

Islands and Tables: Decorative tables or sideboards have no place in the well-designed kitchen because they will become resting places for clutter and because they interfere with smooth traffic flow. The ideal kitchen table not only matches the style of your kitchen, it accommodates the number of people in the household who regularly gather at the table. The shape of the table should suit the shape of the kitchen and leave three or more feet free around the edges for traffic flow. The best kitchen tables are adjustable.

- **Breakfast bars** are tidy, space-saving options for smaller kitchens. If your family usually eats in the dining room, a traditional kitchen table can become a drop zone for clutter. A breakfast bar with stools lets you dine in the kitchen, but is less likely to attract newspapers, hats, gloves, and so forth, because there's simply no room. The breakfast bar can be a freestanding unit in wood or steel, or it can be the edge of an island or kitchen counter.

▲ **Vertical Control** A plain accent pole serves as anchor for innovative hanging storage—adjustable circular shelves that rotate to provide access to seasonings and condiments when needed.

▶ **Island Paradise** This distinctive island is ideal for this narrow kitchen. A larger, more conventional island would have invited clutter and been more difficult to work around. Its role as a combination work surface breakfast bar ensures that any extraneous items are removed promptly from the narrow space to allow food to be prepared and family members to eat.

- **Traditional islands** have solid bases and may include both enclosed and open storage. Be aware that bigger is not necessarily better. Your first consideration will be workspace; the top of the island should be shaped and sized to give you the food-preparation and eating area you need. Then assess how many and what types of items are left over from what you've already stored in cabinets and shelves. Choose an island with cabinets, drawers, or shelves that best accommodate what you need to store in the way in which you want to store it.

- **An island** can be a great place to store seldom-used appliances and kitchen linens. Modern islands increasingly include large, deep, easy-slide drawers that can hold these items. But the kitchen layout must allow enough room for you to stand with the drawer or doors fully open, otherwise the storage will be inaccessible. An excellent alternative to drawers or cabinets is open shelving underneath the island countertop. This not only provides quicker and easier access, it is less expensive and discourages haphazard storage because everything is in plain view.

- **Island alternatives** offer the possibility of specialized storage. Keep an open mind because your needs may be better met by an adapted structure, such as a high table. If you have no need for additional storage, a solid butcher-block surface on four sturdy legs may fill the bill better than a more complex built-in island. It can also be a way to bring a stylistic centerpiece to your kitchen.

- **Seating** in the kitchen follows the same style trend: the simpler the better. Avoid decorative or unused chairs in the kitchen because they're likely to get in the way or be used as places to dump gloves, scarves, and other seasonal clothing that belongs elsewhere. The chairs you use should take up minimal space while still offering comfort.

focus on function

Having chosen the major furnishings for your kitchen, it's time for you to refine your storage and organization with a selection of smaller accessories. Once again, this is an exercise in logic about putting everything near where it will be used. You wouldn't put dish soap on top of the refrigerator, but it's not unusual to see knives or mixing bowls stored far from where food is prepared. You need to reposition things so that they are as close as possible to where they will be used.

Logical Location: Some items, such as cooking utensils, will be specific to a given area. More general supplies, such as canned foods, should be centralized in one convenient

Full Exposure

As visually busy as this kitchen may appear, there is a simple underlying logic to its organization. The layout focuses on placing whatever might be needed exactly where it will be needed, and uses every functional item as a part of the overall décor.

1. All the cooking utensils are kept in a big white jar next to the stove, ready for use at a moment's notice. The informal arrangement is in keeping with the kitchen's theme.

2. Colorful glasses are stored on a handy shelf instead of being hidden away in a cupboard. Shelves often make for easier access and a more appealing display than cabinets. Concealing the glasses in a cupboard would have robbed the kitchen of a splash of color.

3. The brace between the island's poles functions as a hanger rail. Notice that the pots are hung on the stove side so that they can be used when needed for cooking and don't interfere with access to the sink.

4. Baskets are a great way to keep fruit and similar perishables close at hand—in this case, right next to a juicer. Storing these perishables in plain view makes it more likely that they'll get eaten, providing an eye-pleasing way to cut down on spoilage.

5. The island's slotted-wood bottom shelf serves as the storage area for equipment used less often, such as the mixer. Open storage not only keeps these items handy for when they're needed, it also shows off the attractive stainless-steel appliances.

location. Frequently used pots and pans should be stored near the stovetop. Knives, on the other hand, should be near the food-preparation area. Use a magnetic knife strip rather than a knife block, which takes up valuable counter space and harbors bacteria. The food-preparation area should be located near the sink for easy cleanup.

By allowing function to guide the placement of everything in the kitchen, you make using the space that much easier. Ease of use makes keeping things in order a snap. The idea is to give every item in the kitchen a distinct and commonsense "home," which will help ensure that nothing becomes clutter.

Bringing order to the kitchen will involve two types of organizing devices: those you adapt and ready-made solutions available from retailers. Which you choose will depend on your organizational needs and your kitchen's design style.

Manufacturers have made great leaps in creating stylish organizers. Products range from the sleek and modern flair of stainless-steel pot-hanging rods to the more traditional flavor of antiqued ceramic jars for dry goods.

◀ Easy Access Stainless-steel shelving and a long hanging strip reinforce the functional nature of this chef-friendly kitchen. All utensils and knives—and even paper towels—are hung right in front of the user. Dinnerware is arranged attractively on the eye-level shelves, leaving no doubt as to where things belong.

Refer to the four guidelines on page 46 and select products that fit in with your design style. If your taste tends toward the unusual, look to incorporate your own one-of-a-kind solutions, such as using cigar boxes to store napkins and napkin rings. You may also need specialized storage if your kitchen serves as a gathering area where everyone can play cards, read, or do other "family room"-type of activities. No matter what you choose, the goal is to combine practical organization solutions with inviting design.

Suspended Storage: First, consider what can be hung and where, because hanging storage frees up counter space and makes finding utensils and equipment simple and quick. When choosing hanging storage don't limit yourself to products available at retail. For instance, you can outfit a funky, colorful kitchen with a useful hanging bar by mounting a clothes rod between two cabinets. Paint it a color that complements the rest of the kitchen. Or go with a more industrial look by making a pot-hanging rack from cast-iron or coated plumbing pipe. Regardless of the material, the two basic types of hanging storage are wall-mounted and ceiling-mounted.

• Ceiling-mounted structures work best where there is a good deal of clearance and above an existing structure such as an island or a cooktop. Positioned without anything underneath, ceiling-mounted units are jarring to the eye and can impede traffic flow. This type of structure should also be positioned so that the mounting hardware can be fixed into a solid joist, beam, or other structural support.

• **Wall-mounted** styles are more practical in kitchens with low ceilings. Be careful to avoid locating wall-mounted hanging devices where they will obstruct cabinet-door clearance or the opening of drawers.

• **Simple hooks** give you maximum flexibility for hanging all types of items. Hooks allow you to place a single frequently used pot where you want it and they serve as great anticlutter devices. The kitchen is often the entry point for the home and, as such, a place needs to be made for coats and seasonal clothing that never make it to the hall closet. A few hooks by the back door can be a solution.

• **Hooks** can be decorative accents. You'll find them in a panorama of finishes, including brass, chrome, brushed nickel and wood finishes from dark to light. You can also select shapes that reflect the general kitchen design, from ornate curving hooks with filigree for a Victorian kitchen to simple and functional wood hooks for a seaside house.

Storage Containers: What can't be shelved or hung should be kept in stand-alone containers. Containers give you an easy way to store any loose items, from wooden spoons to swizzle sticks to beans, and they are a chance to inexpensively accent the kitchen's design.

The breadth of possible containers is limited only by your imagination. You'll find an incredible mix at retail stores, and that's just the tip of the iceberg. You can adapt an array of containers for use in the kitchen. The key is to use those that fit with the kitchen's décor and efficiently serve your particular storage needs.

• **Glass containers** are a good choice for storing myriad dry goods, from dried beans to brown sugar. The glass reveals the contents at a glance. Styles range from the ornate to the plain, and the material itself is suited to just about any kitchen design scheme. You needn't limit yourself to clear glass; translucent colored glass jars are widely available and clean, used wine bottles with intact corks make wonderful dry-goods containers for staples such as rice and sugar. Just remember that many kitchen staples, such as salt, need to be under an airtight top.

▶ **Tidy Retro** Antique tins liven up this period kitchen with splashes of color and function as unique storage for loose items such as tea bags and dried beans. All other loose items, including the cookware, are kept in the recessed cabinets, allowing the distinctive kitchen design to shine in the neat and tidy space.

SPICING UP YOUR DESIGN

All those little jars of spices can create havoc in your cabinets or drawers. Fortunately, you can choose from a number of chic spice storage options to make them easy to find and nice to look at.

Test-Tube Hangers Although standing-rack versions are available, a wall-mounted rack frees up counter space and places the spices right where they will be used. Both provide a visually interesting display. Test-tube spice racks are best for experienced cooks; labels will quickly fall off the rubber stopper tops or the slick glass tubes, so the cook needs to be able to recognize the spices inside.

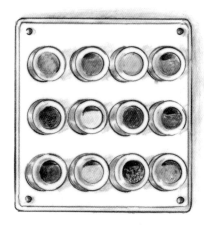

Magnetic Jars A fairly new type of storage, these also fit with just about any kitchen design style. Magnetized metal jars adhere to a base plate that is mounted on a wall. The labels on top of the jars face the user, making spice selection easy. The screw-on lids seal tight to keep spices fresh.

Traditional Spice Racks These come with their own stylized jars or can hold spices in conventional off-the-shelf jars. Choose a countertop version if you have a lot of counter space, otherwise pick a wall-mounted model. The look is distinctive and fits in best with a traditional or country kitchen scheme.

Drawer Inserts A simple spice organizer, it keeps spices at the ready, but hidden away. Each spice sits in a slanted indentation that leaves the label facing out.

- **Metal containers** offer a diversity of options. Stainless steel is an excellent choice that complements most design styles and looks sleek and clean on a countertop or shelf. Add an interesting accent to a country or eclectic kitchen with enameled steel or old-fashioned tin containers. Most metal containers are not airtight and are better for nonperishables such as tea bags or dried pasta. You can even fill sheet-metal magazine racks with catalogs as a fun and funky decorative accent, if you like to relax with a cup of coffee and read at the kitchen table.

- **Painted ceramic** containers come in many different shapes and brightly colored patterns. Although they aren't appropriate for every kitchen, they can add a fun accent to a traditional or period-style design. From cookie jars to the classic quartet of sugar, flour, tea, and coffee canisters, ceramic jars present a cornucopia of options for dry storage. With the lids off, these can also be adapted to store utensils and other kitchen implements.

- **Wood boxes** and trays are excellent for specific uses. Choose a lacquered in-box as a place for homework left on the kitchen table, so your kids always know where to find it. A plain painted box can be used as a place for cold-weather gear that finds its way into the kitchen from the entryway.

◀ **Hidden Assets** A simple
tray and ceramic bowls create
a clutter-fighting composition
on a kitchen table. Most
everything else in this
sophisticated kitchen is hidden
away behind flush-mounted
floor-to-ceiling cabinets—a
good option where utter
simplicity and a streamlined
look are the goals.

productive home workspaces

Less Mess, More Done

industrious enclave

An organized workspace is a vital part of today's home. Whether you actually work full-time at home, occasionally telecommute, or just need to organize your bills and essential paperwork, you need a place dedicated to getting work done. Because most houses aren't built with a designated home-office space, you'll need to create one in an existing room or part of a room. The goal is to smoothly assimilate the home office so that work and the space it takes up don't interfere with the more enjoyable things you do in your home. A correctly designed home office doesn't create disorder or intrude on living spaces, even when it's been carved out of an existing area, such as a nook off a living room.

Getting Down to Business: The challenge is to seamlessly blend the home office with the rest of your décor in a way that prevents clutter. It's a challenge made tougher by technology: there simply aren't a whole lot of color or design options in choosing a computer, printer, fax, or other equipment. And cords running from plugs and between

equipment don't make the predicament any easier. A little thought in selecting your office equipment and furniture—and a little creativity in where and how you place and use those things—can preserve the ever-delicate balance between form and function.

Beyond equipment, the home office is a magnet for paper, and nothing spells mess quite like a tumult of loose paper. Keeping catalogs, flyers, bills, clipped articles, and all the other paperwork life produces in check is a

▶ **Business Incorporated** Meshing perfectly with the room, this incorporated office includes built-in shelves and cabinets that conceal the technology and keep reference works and other supplies neatly and fashionably organized in boxes.

matter of finding innovative workspace storage solutions. The very best clutter-beating options keep papers close at hand, while organizing and concealing them.

Whether you're looking to streamline an existing home workspace, move that space to a more efficient and neater place, or are creating a workspace for the first time, start by looking at all potential locations. Your choice of location will determine the space you have to work with and will guide the other clutter-busting choices you need to make. Then it's just a matter of making sure you have the right furniture, equipment, and organizers for your home and the work you need to do there.

office space

Where you locate your home office is crucial in determining how functional and comfortable it will be. Its location will also affect other areas in the home, as well as determine how simple it will be for you to contain workspace disarray. The choice of location will be guided by the amount of space you need, which depends on three key factors: whether the office is a full- or part-time workspace, the type of work you'll be doing in the office, and the space you have available. For instance, a busy home-based marketing consultant may require a set of bulky filing cabinets, a variety of computer equipment, and a place to hold meetings. All of which call for an entire room.

On the other hand, a simple setup to pay bills and surf the net can require little more than a converted closet or even a corner of a large living room.

Start by assessing how much space you need. Consider the number of books and reference materials you'll use regularly and honestly judge the amount of paper you'll be dealing with. This will help you decide how large your file cabinet will have to be, how much shelf storage you'll need, and whether you'll require extra furniture, such as a printer stand, for equipment. Add to this a reasonable desk and chair and you'll come away with a good idea of how much square footage your office space will take up.

Next look at available areas in the house. The ultimate decision of where to put the office involves balancing the requirements of your home design against your work needs, your family's needs, and the space available. A wide-open living room may feature a small corner or alcove that could be a natural workspace out of the flow of traffic. This could be a great location for a modest setup to deal with work at home one day a week plus household paperwork, mail, and bills. A guest bedroom would be more convenient and appropriate for a complete telecommuting office fully equipped with copier, fax and high-end printer. In any case, keeping the office organized will be easier the less traffic there is around the space.

1 Take Control of Technology: Cables, cords, wires, and peripherals can all create clutter and be visually jarring. Simple strategies and over-the-counter organizers can quickly get your technology in order.

2 Facilitate Workflow: The home office is, after all, about work. Any design or organizational elements you choose should make the space as functional as it is attractive.

3 Keep Papers in Check: Piles of paper are a sure sign of home-office disorganization. Use innovative storage and filing units to handsomely organize your papers where you can quickly and easily find them.

4 Integrate but Define: Your home-office design should blend in with the rest off the house, but it should also have clear boundaries. When you're relaxing in adjacent areas, you shouldn't be bothered by thoughts (or sounds or sights) of work and clutter from other areas shouldn't find its way into the office.

Lofty Workspace

A modern loft provides the background to a functional and well-organized—not to mention suitably sleek—home office.

1 Small steel cups keep pens and pencils centralized, while photos are collected in their own area, with a variety of desktop holders. An expandable steel file holder is used to hold files currently in use.

2 The ample shelving provides spaces of different sizes and shapes for all kinds of reference materials, paperwork, and books. Note the custom "cubby" shelves over the desk work area, keeping small supplies neatly organized and close at hand.

3 Technology is well accommodated with a hole in the desk behind the flat-screen monitor, for cables and power cord, and an underdesk cradle to support the computer itself. A cable channel built into the underside of the desk provides a place for cables hooking the computer to the concealed printer.

4 Files are kept in built-in lateral drawers that are part of the desk unit. A row of standard drawers is positioned within easy reach of the desktop work area.

5 Adding to the other concealed storage, this custom cabinet keeps the printer out of sight, with room for extra printer supplies such as ink cartridges and special papers. The printer sits on a pullout shelf for easy servicing.

▲ **Toil Booth** Integrating a home workspace into an existing room is an exercise in creativity. Here, the office is a converted closet. The built-in desk and shelves are efficient and handsome uses of the space. When not in use, the armless chair slides flush under the desk, and the entire office is concealed behind the closet's original folding doors.

Independent Office If you work full-time at home, or require a lot of computer equipment or silence in your work, you'll need a completely separate office. This is also the appropriate choice for anyone who requires privacy and security in a home office, such as a lawyer who regularly works after hours at home. The independent office requires an entire room or a large portion of an open space such as an attic, allowing you to easily position furniture, storage, and electronic equipment. Good locations for an independent office include a dry basement, an attic with head-room, a spare bedroom, or a den. The challenge in an independent office is setting it up correctly, with the right furniture in the right place. A file cabinet with ample space for papers needs to be close by the desk so that papers get filed before they become clutter. With extra space comes the potential for more clutter, because it's easy to put things aside rather than deal with them. That's why it's wise to use an oversized wastebasket and a large paper-recycling bin so that paper trash doesn't pile up on your desk simply because there is no place else to put it.

◄ **Work Lite** The home workspace should match your needs, and this workspace incorporated into a bedroom provides a very basic sunlit area to pay bills, write letters, and deal with paperwork—no technology required.

orderly innovation

The "Arm's Length Standard" is a good rule to apply when setting up your home office. Basically anything you use on a daily basis should be within an arm's reach of where you sit. This includes desk sets, your in-box, filing cabinet and computer. Those books, papers and equipment you use on a weekly basis should be positioned within a long stretch or short roll of your chair. Items you rarely need to access can be placed much higher up on shelves or farther away.

Separated Workspace If you regularly use your workspace, but have a modicum of paperwork and your equipment is limited to a small computer and printer, your office needs are somewhat more modest. You can opt for a separated workspace, which is an office placed within a larger room but with an element of detachment from the greater space. For instance, a natural nook or alcove makes an excellent site for a separated office, as does a large closet in a big bedroom, the leg of an L-shaped living room, or the space under a wide staircase. These areas provide enough division so that your work area will be outside the general traffic flow but won't take up as much space as an independent office. Outfit the space so that it facilitates the work you need to do there, but use design elements that tie it to the rest of the room. For example, run a row of bookshelves from the office into the room at large to create visual continuity. Use a piece of artwork as a bridge between the

▼ **Blurred Boundaries** This home office space is seamlessly designed into the living room so that it functions as a separated workspace but seems a natural part of the room. A candlestick collection visually joins the office to the rest of the space, as do built-in bookshelves and a desk that matches the colors and textures in the room. The neatly aligned reference books are pleasing to the eye and the large artwork provides a bridge from workspace to relaxation area.

workspace and adjacent area. The drawback to a separated workspace is that any clutter that accumulates will quickly move into the larger room area. That's why you should carefully select effective, convenient small organizers that will stylishly maintain design flow.

▲ **Meeting Place** The home office must accommodate the needs of your business, and this one is well suited to a job that requires meeting and interacting with clients. The surroundings provide an elegant and formal atmosphere conducive to business discussions.

Incorporated Workstation Where there is little space available and you need to do very little work at home, you can simply incorporate a basic workstation into an existing space. This can entail butting a desk against the back of a couch or placing a small desk in the corner of a living room or bedroom. The challenge is keeping this area as spotless as the rest of the room. Incorporated workstations require that you be far more careful in selecting furniture and organization aids. You may also have to adapt how you work. For instance, any kind of file cabinet may seem out of place in a bedroom workstation, so you may want to set up a decorative bin, box, or tray for storing your paperwork to be filed. Then periodically you can take it to wherever the filing cabinet is kept. Choosing a desk material that complements the other surfaces in the room and task lighting that works with the other lighting will make an incorporated workspace seem an integrated part of the décor.

furnishing for productivity

Once you're settled on a location for the home office, you need to think about your work furniture. If you have a desk and shelves you want to use, assess them carefully. The right furniture makes your office setup more efficient, which in turn helps you stay organized. Choose a desk that suits the space and the way you work, handsome storage that provides ample room for work-related books and materials and a file cabinet that will accommodate all your files—now and in the future.

Desk A desk is the central command post of any home office or workspace. The desk you choose needs to fit neatly into the space you've allocated while providing enough surface area to allow you to work unimpeded. A desk that is too large will attract piles of paper. If it's too small it will limit the work you can comfortably do.

orderly innovation

Self-contained offices—all-in-one wardrobe-style pieces with a desk that folds down, interior shelves, and holes and channels for cables—can be wonderful small-space solutions. Placed at one end or in the corner of the room, these units look like simple wardrobes or other pieces of furniture when they are closed. Fully open, however, they are virtually a complete office-in-a-box. Although the design styles are limited, this type of unit can be a quick and easy solution when you feel there is nowhere you can easily incorporate an office workspace into your layout.

▲ **Counter Intelligence** Sometimes an
adapted workspace requires adapted furniture.
In this case, a countertop and cabinetry form a
wonderful quick-access office for a busy interior
designer, who has opted for the convenience
of stools.

▲ **Inside Job** Sometimes customizing a space is the best way to ensure that an office meets your needs. This built-in desk includes a comfortable work corner for computing and paperwork and a span of file cabinet drawers. There's even a drawer for the printer, which stays hidden away when not in use.

- **Desk drawers** can be handy for storing supplies such as paper and notepads, and some large desk drawers are specially equipped to store hanging files. Built-in desks often include large drawers with platforms for a printer, fax, or other equipment. You may also need a desk with locking drawers to store sensitive materials or valuable items. Choose a drawer configuration that suits your needs. For instance, if you use a pull-out underdesk keyboard tray, avoid buying a desk that has a drawer built in that space.

- **Built-in cord** and cable channels are a useful desk feature if your work requires a lot of electronic equipment. These ducts keep cords out of sight and in control, a real plus if your desk is part of an incorporated workstation or is otherwise exposed. They must be planned into the construction of built-in desks.

◀ **Store Galore** An office doubles as a home library, making great use of custom shelving units. The shelves include space for books and decorative pieces, neatly grouped boxes for loose items and concealed storage behind simple colored plastic panels.

▶ **File Flair** Filing cabinets don't have to be dull. This home office includes tall, stacked, freestanding filing cabinets on either side of the desk, featuring wood that matches the desk, and whimsical pulls. Most important, the wealth of storage space offers a place for more than just files.

File Storage Be liberal when judging your file storage needs; extra space in file cabinet drawers can always be put to good use, but a shortage of file space will lead to the chaos of piles of papers with no place to go. In addition to the obvious criterion of pleasing appearance, you'll want to select cabinets based on height. Tall cabinets store more files in a single unit, but two half-height cabinets can store the same number of files, and can be used as supports for a desktop or placed side by side to form a printer stand or a surface for other equipment. Another key consideration is whether the cabinet is stationary or rolling.

91

- **Stationary file cabinets** are constructed of solid wood, laminates with a range of finishes, or painted or unpainted steel. You can even find specialized types with wicker drawers in a wrought-iron frame or translucent plastic drawers. Choose from two basic formats: lateral cabinets in which the files are hung with the front of the files facing to the side, and the more popular vertical cabinets, in which the files are hung facing the front. Most homeowners find vertical types more convenient, because files are easier to read upon opening the drawer. Lateral files require less space to open, which can be an advantage in narrow areas.

- **Rolling file holders** are available in a wider range of styles. Go modern with wire frame units equipped with frosted or brightly tinted plastic drawers. More conventional wood models are available, and you can even turn a stationary filing cabinet into a rolling version with an inexpensive dolly bottom sold to fit standard cabinet measurements. Rolling cabinets can be an excellent choice for the home office. They can be moved where they're needed, then stored out of sight. They also allow you to easily modify the office layout as your needs or preferences change.

orderly innovation

Just like other furniture, filing cabinets can be customized to suit your interior design. Wood cabinets can be sanded and refinished; paint the cabinet white to fit into a country house style or stain it dark to complement a wood-paneled den. Metal cabinets can be stripped and painted any of a number of bright, pastel, or neutral shades (and can even be painted two-tone or checkerboard to fit in with a funkier décor). Or for a rugged look that suits a masculine or industrial office design, strip the cabinet down to the bare metal and finish it with a coat of clear satin acrylic sealer.

Shelves: Shelves are an indispensable addition to any home workspace, providing a place for books, magazines, supplies, and equipment such as scanners. Built-in shelves are a better option for small confined spaces, such as a converted closet. Freestanding shelves are good options for larger areas and in exposed spaces, where the décor may change over time. However, shelves can also become cluttered, making it harder to find what you need when you're at work. Consequently, loose objects on a shelf should be stored in a labeled container such as a box. Organize everything on your office shelves in groups according to use (e.g., different types of printer paper in one place, all reference books in a row, etc.).

▲ **Shelf Satisfying** Built-in shelves help keep this home workspace tidy. In addition to reference books, the shelves hold a number of decorative boxes labeled with their contents.

technology

Computers, fax machines, and other electronics have become indispensable fixtures in many home offices. The majority of American homes have a computer, printer, and Internet connection, and an increasing number have a scanner, copier, and other peripheral devices.

All these machines can increase work efficiency, make day-to-day chores easier, and even make life more enjoyable. But technology can also increase clutter exponentially. All this equipment needs a place to go, and some objects, such as printers, take up even more space in use. Their cords alone can be a nightmare, and small peripheral devices and supplies such as paper and printer cartridges, can create a profoundly disorderly situation if they are not properly organized. In setting up your workspace, you need to account for all the equipment—and attendant supplies— you'll use.

◀ **Cord Free** The layout of this posh home office includes a large desk, a comfortable sitting area for meetings, tons of windows, and few power outlets. Wireless equipment makes it all work. The laptop on the desk functions as the homeowners' main computer, and the printer, out of view, is wireless as well. Even the Internet connection is wireless, allowing the computer to be used throughout the house.

▶ **Technocozy** A compact workstation is situated in a hallway dogleg to be near the phone jack and power outlet. The homeowner has created a paperless space and uses a simple computer setup to write reports, correspond via e-mail, and do spreadsheet bookkeeping.

Computers and Monitors: If you have a standard desktop computer you should determine where to keep the computer tower so that it is out of the way. If there's room, use a computer trolley or stand to keep it under the desk. If you have peripherals, such as external hard drives or a cable modem, use a trolley with shelves or compartments for the peripherals. A smaller computer can serve as a base for a lightweight monitor. Monitors can be space hogs, so if you're buying new or upgrading, get a flat-panel unit that will take up less space. If you type a lot, invest in a sliding platform that will position the keyboard and mouse at optimum height and out of the way under the desk when not in use.

Printers: These are key players in today's home office. Smaller models can be placed on the desktop or on a deep shelf. But if you have a more sophisticated printer or do a lot of printing, you'll probably want to dedicate a surface to the printer. Be sure to select a location that allows adequate room for both the paper feed and output tray, so that paper doesn't wind up falling on the floor every time you print. This can be the top of a file cabinet or an independent printer stand that provides storage for paper, ink cartridges, and other supplies. As a general rule, keep printer supplies as close to the printer as possible.

Copiers: Like printers, copiers require extra space for the movement of paper—and sometimes parts of the copier itself—during operation. Because copiers are not normally connected to other pieces of equipment, they can be put on independent stands, just about anywhere in the office as long as they are near a power source. If you use the copier infrequently, position it out of the way, far from the desk.

orderly innovation

Laptop computers are increasingly replacing desktop models as the technology of choice for home offices. Advances in laptops mean that these portable units are often just as powerful as desktop systems. Manufacturers have also increased the quality and size of laptop screens so that they rival desktop monitors in resolution and graphic ability. All of which makes the laptop a great home workspace choice, one that eliminates the clutter of separate pieces of equipment and all the cables that come with them.

Scanners: These handy pieces of equipment have become a favorite in the home office as a way to quickly format images to be sent via e-mail or placed in documents. The scanner should be placed near the computer to shorten the distance the cable needs to span and for ease of use. If you use it often, make room for the scanner on the surface of your desk. If you rarely use it, disconnect it between uses and keep it on a shelf.

Fax and Phones: Basic communication devices are essential tools for the home workspace. Usually a phone will suffice and you merely need to clear a space on the desktop for the phone. If you include a fax, you'll need a place for it with the same space requirements as a printer or copier, because of the need for a paper feed and output. You should also dedicate a box or tray to incoming faxes so that they are kept in order. Lines for the phone and/or fax should be run from the nearest phone jack. If you have to run a long phone line, secure it to the baseboard with clips meant for this purpose (available from hardware stores and home centers).

Controlling Cables: Power cords and cables going from your computer to other equipment can make for unattractive visual clutter. If your computer desk did not come with built-in cord channels, look for a flexible conduit that captures all your cords in one group and that can be attached to the underside of your desk or other surfaces with adhesive fasteners or screw-in clips. Office-supply stores and home centers offer many other cable-controlling accessories, from small plastic brackets with individual channels to easily removable fasteners that bunch cords together. You can also improvise by using twist ties or other fasteners to gather cables into a manageable bundle.

Wireless Technology: Almost all modern computers have some wireless capability, commonly known as WiFi. This technology allows you to avoid cables altogether and gives you much more freedom in where you position computers and peripherals. You can free up your keyboard and mouse with wireless versions, eliminate the cord to your printer, and use a wireless hub for your Internet connection.

workspace aids: organizers and accessories

Turn to the vast variety of desktop, shelf, and independent organizers to keep your workspace in order. Always select such accessories based on what you need to store. They must be correctly sized for your needs or they will simply add to your clutter problems.

In-Boxes: Even the most basic home office should have an in-box or tray, and sometimes more than one. A standard in-box can also be a place to keep papers that need to be filed or dealt with when you get time. In-boxes provide a way to personalize your workspace with accents that create style. Use a steel jeweler's tray, a silver serving dish, or a regular wire inbox. The only requirement is that the box be larger than 8½" × 11". Choose stackable versions to organize different types of paperwork.

Mail organizers serve the same function as a regular in-box, but they are dedicated to keeping mail and bills organized. The most useful mail organizers include a tray for loose mail, a slotted shelf to keep bills in order, and small compartments for stamps and envelopes.

General Utensils Organizer: Every desk needs a place for pens, pencils, scissors, tape, letter opener, and the other small items that you use day to day. Keep these close at hand with one general desktop caddy. Caddies and carousels are available at office-supply stores and come in many different materials, from plastic to wood to steel. If you rarely use some of these tools, employ a desktop pen set and keep other items, such as rulers and staplers, on a shelf or in a drawer where you can quickly reach them.

style file

Keep CDs and DVDs in a container that improves the look of your home workspace. CD wallets come in various sizes (depending on capacity) and are available in leather, fabrics, and other pliable materials. Some have rigid spines that allow them to sit upright on a shelf, like a book. You can also opt for a more high-tech look by buying a CD suitcase in a stainless-steel or rigid plastic outer shell.

▲ Modest Labor

A business owner uses this simple workspace—
a desk abutting a living room couch—as a quiet
space where he can catch up on calls and reading away from his busy office. When he needs a
computer link, he uses a laptop with a wireless
connection.

FINE FILING OPTIONS

Even if you only use your home workspace for bill paying and organizing your personal affairs, you'll need a filing cabinet. Although the type you choose will depend somewhat on available space, the options are varied enough that you should be able to pick a file cabinet that suits your décor as well.

Sturdy Classic The most common filing cabinets are the basic and functional vertical types. Available in differing heights of two, three, or four drawers, these come in metal or wood finishes. Use a pair of two-drawer units as supports for a simple desktop.

Sideways Lateral file cabinets are not as deep as vertical files because the files sit sideways in the drawers. This makes them ideal for tight areas where they can placed against a wall like a side table. This type is also available in two- or four-drawer configurations, and in metal and wood finishes.

Moving Papers Sometimes mobility can be a blessing, and a file cabinet you can easily move from one spot to the other can be essential in a home office with tight space. Although you can use special dollies designed for box-type filing cabinets, wheeled file trolleys are a more stylish option. Choose from simple frame-and-caster models with a minimal look, or keep papers from falling out of the side with a model constructed with solid sides.

Shelf-ish Proposition If a cabinet is more than you need, or you want to avoid adding a standalone structure to your home office setup, use a file holder. Essentially boxes with rails for the hanging folder hooks, these can be placed on a shelf, shoved under the desk or kept on top. And you don't have to sacrifice style because they come in a range of materials, from steel wire to fabric to wood.

SPECIALIZED STORAGE

These days, there is a storage container that can bring order to any of the naturally chaotic elements in the office, such as loose magazines or odd-shaped supplies. And you need not rely solely on commercially available products. For instance, use the elegant, sturdy boxes expensive stores provide with sweaters or other garments to hold your inventory of office supplies.

Standing Tall Magazine cases—sturdy vertical boxes made to sit upright on a shelf—bring order to more than just magazines. Taking up a minimum of shelf space, they can be used to hold computer manuals and professional journals, catalogs and flyers. The selection includes colored plastic, wire mesh, wood, and metal types.

Boxing Match Boxes can be the catch-all solution for keeping supplies and small accessories in order on a shelf, the top of a cabinet, or right on your desktop. You can find storage boxes made to fit on standard shelf depths at office supply stores. Or take a more stylish route and shop for boxes at an art-supply store. Choose from colored translucent plastic cases to keep extra staples and paper clips organized, or pick a large box with a pull or cut out handle to keep extra cords, cables, and peripherals in one handy location.

Slipped Disk Computer CDs, DVDs, and other disks can be stored out of sight in a box, but if you use them regularly, you should keep them exposed in a standing or mounted rack. Use a wood, metal, or plastic rack that matches the office décor, and buy a rack or racks that accommodate more than the number of disks you have.

detailed dining rooms

Stylish Storage in the
Least-Used Room

memorable meals

The dining room is often the most specialized room in the house; its sole purpose is to accommodate meals small and large, from special occasions to everyday dinners. This singular role can be a blessing and a curse. On the plus side, you don't have to plan for multiple purposes or the different needs of people with a legitimate claim on the space. But a dining room can become an organizational challenge when people start using it for other purposes. That's how you wind up with left-behind homework, unopened mail, discarded jackets, and other clutter making a mess of the room.

Design for Dining: Organizing a dining room for the long term means designing to defend it against casual incursions of clutter from other rooms. Whether your dining room is a separate formal room or a wide-open area off the kitchen it needs to be designed to deter any use but dining.

In organizing this room, it's a good idea to start by pulling out everything currently stored there so you know what you need to plan for. If you're like a lot of people, your dining room closet or hutch probably holds at least a few items you haven't seen or thought about in years. Either give away or store unwanted gifts and other items you're not likely to use. Next assess whether you have the right storage furniture for the tableware, serving pieces, and accessories you need to keep on hand. That assessment will direct you in your choice of a control piece or pieces—your essential storage and display furniture.

▶ **Big Blockers** A trio of oversized vases not only serves as a unique decorative display in this formal dining room, it also blocks most of the table's surface area, intimidating anyone from casually placing odds and ends there.

1 Block Table Clutter: The surface of a dining room table is an inviting place to dump just about anything. Stop unwanted clutter by keeping the table partially or completely set with place settings.

2 Focus on Dining: If it does not have something to do with serving, eating, or enjoying food and drink, it doesn't belong in the dining room.

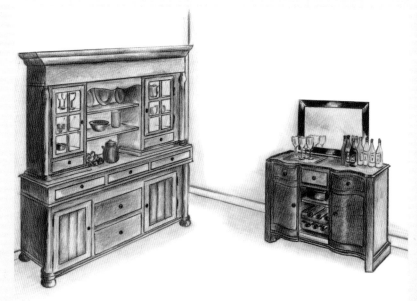

3 Display Special Pieces: Serving dishes, decorative plates, and sterling-silver pieces are just a few of the functional objects that can be placed on display to become part of the décor. This frees up room inside drawers and cabinets.

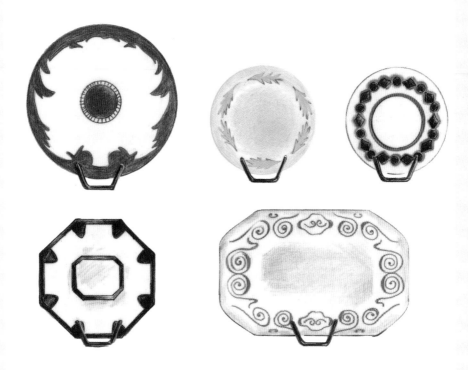

the control piece

Every well-organized dining room needs a "control piece" of furniture that serves as a command center for storage and meals. Depending on your style, this may be a low, long, sleek art nouveau sideboard or a contemporary tall and broad oak hutch. It may also be a combination of pieces, such as a corner cabinet with glass doors and a side table with cabinets underneath and open space on top. Ideally, whatever you use as your control piece should offer a mix of functions, including exposed storage, concealed storage, and space to set down food and beverages that can't be put on the table for one reason or another.

Exposed Storage: So much of what you keep on hand in the dining room is beautiful in its own right. Crystal, china, silver vessels, and serving sets are just a few of the dining room accessories that are as decorative as they are useful; they deserve to be visible. Two types of exposed storage are glass-fronted cabinets and open storage, such as shelves.

- **Glass-door cabinets** allow you to neatly display your favorite serving pieces while protecting them from breakage and keeping them away from dust. To make dining room glassware or dishes easy to get to and appealing to look at align them in tidy

▲ **Wood Works** A sturdy, classic Arts & Crafts sideboard provides varied storage and functions as an ideal control piece. Different size drawers offer plenty of flat storage, with raised-panel cabinets for larger and visually uninteresting pieces. The top surface is decorated with a vase, lamp, and tea set, all of which can be moved aside to make room for serving dishes during meals. An under-shelf ledge serves as a place for plates and other accessories.

▶ **Clean Scene** The top of a table in this elegant dining room is kept pristine with the help of high-back chairs, a long table runner, and centerpieces that combine to block the placement of clutter.

OPEN BAR

Part of regular entertaining is keeping a well-stocked bar. The challenge lies in storing the bottles, which are often too tall for existing shelves, and are prone to tipping over. Stored out in the open on top of a sideboard or on the serving surface of a hutch, bottles of different spirits can get in the way when it comes time to serve dinner. The best answer is often a stand-alone bar unit.

Bar Trolley A bar trolley cart can be a great way to organize liquor bottles and mixers, along with highball and other glasses. You can use a trolley as an accent piece—choosing among several different styles from contemporary glass-and-chrome types to antique wood models. Make sure it has wheels, because it's handy to be able to entertain in other rooms and roll the trolley out of the way when necessary.

Bar Globe For a classic accent to a formal dining room, consider a bar globe. This turn-of-the-century traditional fixture appears to be a large representation of the world, but opens up to reveal a small bar, with a limited number of bottles and glasses. It can be a very sophisticated way to entertain in a dramatic dark wood dining room.

Liquor Cabinet As a complement to the control piece in your dining room, a liquor cabinet becomes both a design accent and functional furnishing. This traditional piece usually comes with plenty of storage in the cabinet area for a good supply of alcohol, and has ledges or compartments for glassware. The top surface is handy for mixing cocktails and as an overflow surface for big meals with many serving dishes.

Bar Hutch If you have a large dining room and entertain quite often, a bar hutch might serve your adult beverage needs better than smaller units. This is a full-sized service piece, available in the same range of styles as a sideboard or standard hutch. Bar hutches offer plentiful storage for stemware and other glasses, a serving area with lots of elbow room for mixing and pouring, room enough for a full complement of liquor bottles, and even amenities such as a wine refrigerator.

▲ **Side Show** A cord-front sideboard complements latticework chairs and cord-wrapped table
legs. It boasts a large top surface for hot dishes
or storage of large serving vessels. The glass-front
cabinets below hold a full complement of dinnerware and companion pieces.

◄ **Hanging Around** Delicate teacups hang
from individual hooks under these wall-mounted
shelves. Creating a colorful composition, the
shelves hold a multitude of dishes, bowls, glasses
and plates. Notice how the pieces are positioned
with enough room between them to allow for
access and to prevent breakage.

rows with room enough between each glass so that you can comfortably remove one without risking breakage. You can simply stack dishes, but they look nicer in a dish organizer that will store them upright on their sides. Stacking tea cups increases the risk of breakage, so either align them in rows or hang them from hooks on the underside of a shelf. The goal in positioning anything in glass-fronted cabinets is to create a pleasing composition that allows easy access to the pieces.

• Open storage includes shelving that can be integral to a piece of furniture such as a hutch, a freestanding shelving unit or wall-mounted—and the top surfaces of furniture. Exposed shelves are excellent for larger pieces such as serving bowls or pitchers. The top of a shorter piece such as a sideboard can be a great place to keep decorative items that are regularly used in the dining room, including candlesticks and flower vases. The top of taller furnishings such as hutches and cabinets is good for large serving pieces such as punch bowls.

Concealed Storage: The dining room must also house items that are not decorative or too large to be stored out in the open. For these you need a certain amount of storage that is out of sight. The types of concealed

dining room storage include enclosed cabinets, drawers, and boxes you can place on a shelf or in a cabinet. Each is best suited for storing different types of items.

▲ Solid Citizen This sturdy sideboard contains cutlery and other silverware in shallow drawers, with space in large lower cabinets for serving pieces and other fine-dining necessities. The top of the sideboard is a stage for a large decorative vase and an oversized silver bar tray, complete with glassware, ice bucket, and decanters. Decorative platters find a home perched on a plate rail.

- **Drawers** are ideal for linens such as napkin sets and extra tablecloths and for silverware. Store linens with a cedar block or sprigs of lavender to deter insects. Your sterling silver, including large serving pieces, should be kept in antitarnish cloth bags, whether stored in their own boxes or loose. If you are storing your silver in a drawer, keep it away from other hard items that could bump or scratch it. Drawers are also a good place for flat serving trays and oversized chargers that may not comfortably fit on shelves.

- **Cabinets** provide concealed storage for larger items, such as big serving bowls and larger serving baskets and trays. A cabinet can also be a place to conceal a small bar setup, or extra linens and supplies such as candles. However, don't let the cabinet space become a blind space that falls into disarray. Make sure that everything stored in a cabinet is given plenty of room. Keep in mind that fine table linens need to breathe and should not be placed in direct contact with wood or sterling silver. It's best to keep them in acid-free boxes inside the cabinet; label the boxes and make sure you can easily get them in and out. You want to make setting and clearing the dining table as simple as possible.

- **Boxes** can add decorative accents to the dining room while concealing supplies such as extra candles or light bulbs for a chandelier. The advantage of boxes is that you can match the size of the box precisely to whatever it is you need to store—and the box style to your décor. Use a wicker basket with a lid for a collection of special placemats and napkin rings or an antique tin box to hold a set of demitasse cups and saucers. Let your imagination be your guide.

Serving Surface: Every control piece needs some accessible, flat open space that can be used to hold platters of food, chilled bottles of wine in buckets, and other meal-related items that don't fit on the table. The surface can be decorated with accents such as a bowl of fruit or special-occasion candlesticks, but you should leave enough room so that nothing needs to be moved out of the way when placing platters or bowls of food.

orderly innovation

Although your fine china makes for lovely display, it's better protected when concealed because china requires special care to prevent chipping. Always use a buffer between plates. For more secure storage, keep china in special padded boxes made for that purpose; these come in a variety of sizes.

▲ **Kitchen Aid** Sometimes a control piece doesn't need to be big to be effective. This dining room is an integrated part of an open layout, situated between kitchen and living room. The close proximity of the kitchen and its abundant storage means that a simple four-drawer sideboard is all that's needed in the dining room—everything but fine linens and silver can be stored in the kitchen cabinets. The kitchen also supplies serving surfaces, leaving the sideboard top free to function as a bar.

the table

Your dining room table is an irresistible magnet for clutter. Whether as a place to dump mail on the way through the room or a temporary resting area for books on their way back to the library, dining room tables just seem to call out to all the odds and ends in the house. The first line of defense against disorder is to make the open surface area as small as possible. If your table has removable leaves, take them out and store them when you're not serving large dinners. Centerpieces are an essential part of the clutter-busting strategy, and you should keep one on the table at all times. Your centerpiece should reflect your personal style. It's also smart to keep the table covered with a tablecloth or other protective covering to prevent scratches. Lastly, use place settings as protection against clutter. If you don't wish to keep the table set in its entirety, you can just set out placemats, chargers or single plates, with napkins attractively arranged across them. Or go simple with white bowls centered on basic fabric placemats. Whatever you choose to use as placeholders, your aim is to prevent anyone from setting things down around the edges of the table.

Chairs: Dining room chairs can also be magnets for clutter. Whenever possible, store extra dining chairs out of the room so that they don't become parking places for boxes, clothes, and other items that belong elsewhere. If you have the wall space and plenty of room to move around the table (and like the look), you can hang chairs from sturdy hooks on the wall.

orderly innovation

Using boxes for storage can be your chance to accessorize the dining room with small touches of style or color that will bring the space to life. The assortment of decorative yet useful boxes available is simply astounding. You can choose from sophisticated fabric options such as boxes wrapped in raw silk, or try an Asian look with filigreed wood boxes. Bring a raw-edged look to a funky or modern dining room with sheet-metal storage boxes. Whatever style you choose, always buy the box size to suit the storage need, not the other away around.

▶ **Nook Neatness** Sharing a dining alcove with a shelf unit full of reference material, this dining table needs to combat potential paper clutter making its way from the shelves to the tabletop. The curved sides and the fact that the table is left with place settings in position at all times ensure that it is never mistaken for a work surface.

▲ **Small Wonder** Small interiors call for an economy of furnishings, which leads to simple, clutter-free areas. This compact dining table is positioned out of the path of traffic. There's limited room on top for odds and ends, and the stools slide neatly underneath so that they don't become resting places for jackets, scarves, and other garments.

▶ **Serape Style** The table in this Southwestern dining room has been covered with a red table-cloth, a trick that discourages clutter from being put on the tabletop. The room also features an imposing Mission-style hutch that offers copious concealed storage, with shelves that display decorative plates. The bottom half of the hutch includes a broad serving surface.

additional storage

The pieces of furniture that comprise your dining room suite may not accommodate all the things you need to store. You may have extra sets of plates or serving platters or too many supplies to fit in your drawers. In this case, you'll need to turn to other storage options.

Closet: A closet in or near the dining room is the best place for extra leaves that you take out of the table and for keeping table pads if you use them. A closet is also great for long-term storage of items you rarely use, such as seasonal serving sets that come out only at Christmas or Thanksgiving, or special decorations for events such as birthdays. If your closet is large enough, you can also use it to stack extra chairs, to keep them out of the flow of traffic. In smaller dining rooms, closets can be equipped with extra shelves to accommodate a variety of little-used servers, centerpieces, and other items that are best kept out of view.

Mounted Storage: Once you have exhausted all your other storage options, turn to shelves and flat racks that mount on the wall. Shelves should be mounted so that they

▲ **Stand Out** A long sideboard serves as the single storage piece in a narrow dining room. Individual stands showcase the serving platters on top, keeping them organized in the process.

are not in the way of people moving around the table. Flat storage racks fastened to the wall allow you to display decorative plates, saucers, and serving dishes. "Hidden support" racks allow plates and platters to appear to float on the wall, while decorative holders such as wrought-iron racks create an attractive framework for your display.

Wine Racks: Ideally wine should be kept in a cool dark place; after your basement or an actual wine refrigerator, a dining room closet

◄ **Turn Table** High-back chairs enclose a modest dining table with an oversized centerpiece grouping of candles. All combine to make the table inaccessible for anything but dining, preventing clutter build-up.

Storage Space

- A pair of built-in cabinets with solid doors provide extra storage for any large objects that are commonly used for entertaining but that the homeowner doesn't want to put on display.

- Another built-in cabinet, this time with glass-front doors, provides a place to store glassware and other prized possessions. The counter beneath is an ideal space to set serving dishes during a formal meal or to accommodate a bar on informal occasions.

- Hidden behind the table is a custom banquette with a glass table that can be used for break- fast or any other time the homeowners are not entertaining a crowd.

- A wrought-iron chandelier with a large vase centered beneath it draws the focus of the dining room to the table, defining the purpose of the room. It also helps the home- owner defend against incursions of homework, bills, and other clutter.

may be the best location. If you decide to keep a few bottles out in the open, you'll find many innovative racks to choose from, some wall-mounted and some freestanding. Some hutches and sideboards have built-in wine cubbies. Choose wine storage that fits with your dining room décor and can be put in a logical and safe place. Conventional wall-mounted racks—those that position the bottle pointing out—are quite deep and may get in the way of people walking around the room. If you want a mounted unit, consider a rack that allows the bottles to be positioned parallel to the wall. If you'd prefer a rack to sit on the sideboard or other surface, buy one that has a relatively small footprint so that you'll still have plenty of room for oversized bowls and serving plates during meals.

▲ **Feeling Blue** A tiered stand helps keep a collection of pitchers in order, while matching platters are hung on the wall with individual wire hangers—they're essentially functional decoration that reduces the need for other storage.

style file

Wine racks add a wonderful visual focal point to the dining room. The diversity of wine storage units is vast and varied. Traditional wall-mounted boxes with cubbies for the bottles compete with wrought-iron racks meant to sit on top of a sideboard. But you can also buy a freestanding steel "tower" that supports the bottles by their necks and fits neatly into a corner.

tidy
bathrooms

Chic and Cozy Solutions

the small busy space

A bathroom is usually the most active room in the house. Typically, it must accommodate several different people, for a variety of purposes, often within a short period of time. Couple this frenetic bustle with the relatively small size of the room, and the opportunity for chaos becomes all too apparent.

Form and Function: The process of protecting your bathroom against the onslaught of clutter begins with your choice of bathroom furnishings. Start by looking at the key areas of sink, vanity, medicine chest, and the toilet and tub regions; solutions in these important areas will go a long way toward effectively streamlining and reorganizing the room. Although you may not want to change your sink or vanity, in some cases it can be converted to accommodate different types of stylish storage. Or you may decide to incorporate new storage in the form of cabinets, shelves, racks, or freestanding units, which are available at relatively modest prices and in various sizes.

Once you've equipped your bathroom with the right furnishings, you'll need to bring in all the supporting players as well—organization aids that complement the vanity, cabinets, or étagère. In such a small space, even something as simple as a towel bar, a modest set of glass containers, or a strategically placed shelf

▲ **Dual Identity** His-and-her sinks can make a couple's bathroom exponentially more useful, but also require double the organization. This tidy setup includes a simple center dresser with plenty of drawer space, replacing medicine cabinets, undersink vanity space, and towel closet.

can have a substantial effect on the room and how it's used. Start at the sink, but look at every available object and surface in the bathroom to find the mix of storage options that will make the space as efficient and attractive as possible.

▲ **Stand Alone** It's best to have towels where you need them, especially when the tub or shower is far from any wall-mounted bar. In this case, a freestanding towel rack is the best option, especially one with multiple bars for plenty of hanging space. The back bars are used for clean towels, the front for drying used towels.

1 Control Towels: Keeping towels off the floor of the bathroom (and other rooms) means you need a place to put not only dry, clean towels but also wet ones and those that are ready for the laundry.

2 Provide Storage: Choose from the available options to ensure that, no matter how small, your bathroom always has adequate and appropriate storage. Without it, clutter will become a constant problem.

3 Contain: The secret to keeping clutter and disorder out of the bathroom is to keep all the small loose items that are used there in separate containers.

sink story

Bathroom organization begins with your sink because unlike the other installed fixtures— toilet, bath, and shower stall—a sink can take many different forms. The type of sink you have or are willing to install will ultimately affect how much additional storage space you will need in other areas of the bathroom. Although there are many different styles of sink, the four basic forms are pedestal, console, wall-mounted, and vanity sinks. Each has its own advantages and disadvantages.

Pedestal: These are two-piece units with a column base that supports a basin. Some pedestal sinks include modest shelves built into the base, but the vast majority offer no storage capacity. Generally, the sink-top area is limited as well. But because these types of sinks take up a minimum of room, they are ideal for powder rooms, where little storage is required, or smaller bathrooms where floor space precludes the use of a vanity. In most cases, you'll need to use shelves or a slim, over-the-toilet étagère in place of the storage you would have with a vanity.

Console: Similar to pedestal sinks, console units support a basin with two front legs and a wall mount, or a full four-leg frame. They present opportunity for storage in the open space beneath the sink and along the frame where

one exists. Braces of a sink frame can serve as towel racks for hand towels, or put a basket under the sink to hold extra rolls of toilet paper or extra towels.

▲ **Clutter-Free** This country-style bathroom makes the most of available space, combining the flair of a clawfoot tub with the utility of a multipurpose vanity. Side shelves give the vanity great towel capacity, and accent containers are put to excellent use on the vanity top. These mesh baskets keep soft goods in view and are right at home in the bright white décor.

Wall-mounted Sinks: In vogue for their sophisticated appearance, wall-mounted sinks offer far less storage than other types of bathroom sinks. With scant (sometimes no) sink-top room, they do however allow for a complete storage unit to be placed underneath. This can be anything from a wicker hamper to a glass-and-chrome cabinet.

Vanity: Vanities are framed cabinets with a top surface into which the sink is set. Depending on the vanity, they may offer storage in the form of an under-sink cabinet, drawers, the sink-top area for exposed items and, less often, open shelving. If you're thinking about changing your sink and vanity, consider what type of storage you need. In a bathroom used by several people, abundant concealed storage is often handy for extra supplies such as toilet paper, cotton pads and swabs, extra boxes of tissue, and other utilitarian items.

▼ **Vanity Space** In a large shared bathroom, finding storage enough to accommodate everyone can be a challenge. That challenge is met in this bathroom with a vanity complete with centerpiece dresser, allowing for towels large and small, backup supplies, personal care products, and much more.

SELECTING SINK TYPES

The style of mounting determines the type of sink and the look of the whole sink area.

Above-Counter Sink Above-counter sinks sit atop the vanity or sink ledge, connected at their base where the drain runs down to the waste pipe. Above-counter sinks are often varied in shape to take advantage of the exposure. Available shapes include teardrop, square, and asymmetrical, among others.

Drop-In Sink Drop-in sink bowls are the traditional style for a vanity, sitting relatively flush with the surrounding surface. Although not particularly distinctive, they allow a vanity or top surface to shine as the focal point.

Wall-Mount Sink Wall-mount sinks don't require a pedestal or vanity because the whole unit bolts to the wall. These sinks are constructed to hide the drainpipe and to "float" against the wall, in a sophisticated modern look. They come in various shapes, some with a top surface built in, others just as a bowl.

Semicountertop Sink

Semicountertop sinks sit just above the surrounding surface, projecting upward one to three inches. This provides the appearance of relief without the sink bowl being the entire focal point. This type is usually round or oval, with or without ornamented lips.

Undercounter Sink Where the vanity or sink surface should be in the spotlight, consider an undercounter sink. These types are sunk below the surface of the vanity or ledge, making them seem deeper than the average sink. This style can be used only with solid countertops or surfaces, because the edge of the sink cutout is exposed.

STUNNING SINKS

Contemporary sink options extend to very sophisticated models in unusual materials that are almost works of art in some cases, and are always attention-getters. These are generally offered as above-counter basins to best show off their unique appearances.

1 Glass sinks represent a high-tech style that goes well with a steel frame and modernistic faucets. Choose from fused, cast, or other kiln-shaped glass bowls in a variety of sizes and in every color of the rainbow, ranging from opaque to translucent.

2 Custom painting brings a whole new face to the common porcelain sink. Painted with images in an array of styles from pure abstraction to delicate, realistic florals, these sinks invite long hand-washing sessions.

3 Get back to nature with marvelous stone sinks. Stone sinks come in almost every type of rock found in nature and a range of surface textures. Choose from smooth marble, finished granite, rough soapstone, and more. Stone sinks go well with other colors and textures from nature, such as rich deep greens and browns and fiber wall coverings.

4 If unique is what you seek you could do a lot worse than a metal sink. Choose stainless, hammered steel or other metal in finishes from high-gloss to brushed. Or go with an extremely distinctive look by using unfinished copper, letting the moisture create a green patina over time.

- **Vanity cabinets** come in all shapes and sizes, ranging from simple box-style cabinets to units with drawers, shelves and cabinet space combined. The simplest vanities feature generous unfinished space inside, but you can buy one with shelves—or install shelves—inside the cabinet to give you the most flexibility in what you store there. The best way to keep things in order in a vanity cabinet is to use containers for all loose times grouped by type, such as cleaning supplies or backup bath and shower products.

orderly innovation

Adaptation can be the best way to find unusual organizers for the top of the vanity. Where simple surfaces and faux-stone-textured walls set a tone for the bathroom use bricks with holes in them to hold toothbrushes and razors. Or use decorative steel trays to organize your makeup. Let the style of your bathroom and the amount of storage you need guide your imagination in finding innovative organizers for bathroom storage.

- **The type** of vanity you choose depends largely on your available space and bathroom style. You'll find vanities in a multitude of designs, including antique or country style, with or without legs, opulent marble versions, and even sleek, all-glass modern versions. If you have plenty of storage space elsewhere in the bathroom, you might opt for a simple console with legs and open space underneath. This is a clean look that allows you to slide a shelving unit on wheels underneath if your storage needs grow.

- **Drawers** provide more specialized storage for the various odds and ends that are used in the bathroom. If your vanity has drawers, make your life easier by installing drawer organizers that keep the contents in order. Specialized organizers are available for such things as cosmetics and dental-care items.

- **Vanity-top surfaces** can be valuable real estate in the bathroom; you just have to be careful not to clutter the surface with loose items such as tubes of toothpaste or shaving supplies. The number-one rule for vanity and sink-top surfaces is to contain anything you put there. For instance, if you want to keep makeup supplies on the sink top, keep them in a decorative box with enough room to completely conceal the cosmetics when you're not using them. Vanity-top containers not only serve as efficient organizers, they

also give you the opportunity to accent your bathroom décor with splashes of color or unusual box shapes or materials. Keep in mind that, as with other decorative elements, vanity-top containers should complement one another; too many or extremely contrasting styles will look jarring. The containers should also be waterproof.

▲ **Sink Strategy** Even a basic frame-supported sink can serve an organizing role. The chrome pipe frame of this stylish model serves as a towel rack. Above the basin, a glass shelf with chrome rail keeps small toiletries in order.

condensing the medicine chest

Almost every bathroom has one, and they are almost always overloaded. Medicine chests can add to clutter when they become too full to hold what should naturally go in them. When there's no room for dental floss or cough syrup in the medicine chest, those items inevitably get shuttled to the surface of the vanity or a nearby shelf. That's why a crucial step in organizing the bathroom is to go through your medicine chest and remove everything that is not absolutely necessary. Dispose of all expired medicines. Next make sure that whatever is kept in the medicine chest fits and belongs there. If a large bottle of mouthwash needs to be jammed in on an angle, you need to find another place to put it. Backup supplies such as bars of soap and extra boxes of cotton swabs are better located in another area of the bathroom. If after this purge you find that your medicine chest is still overloaded, you may want to consider adding a wall-mounted cabinet to the bathroom.

▲ **Sink Storage** You don't need a vanity for effective undersink storage. A simple wooden frame with a bottom shelf serves as useful storage for a bevy of easily accessible rolled towels.

Informal Order

A casual décor doesn't have to mean clutter. This neat and orderly bathroom incorporates user-friendly organization aids throughout.

1 The pedestal sink is much more streamlined than a vanity base, making it a better fit with this light and airy space. The modest sink-top surface prevents clutter—there's simply very little area in which to set something down.

2 A small glass shelf offers just enough space for folded hand towels and toothbrushes kept in a rinse cup.

3 Basic and attractive hooks keep festive guest towels within reach of the sink and ensure that they air-dry quickly.

4 Protruding soap dishes and hanging shower caddies can get in the way and are hard to clean in the bath. These built-in niches are much more aesthetically pleasing and useful.

5 The folding stool serves many roles in the informal bathroom. It can supply a platform for extra towels or bath sponges, give a bather space for a mug of tea and a book or magazine, and even function as a handy seat for applying toenail polish.

6 A "mini-vanity" unit combines shelves and drawer to provide much the same amount of usable storage a regular vanity would, but in more compact form. Its portability allows for easy cleaning and relocation as necessary.

141

towel turnover

The more people there are using the bathroom, the more towels become an organizational challenge. First, you have to create enough storage for dry towels so that everyone using the bathroom has a fresh one when they need it. But you also have to be sure to provide a convenient drying place for wet towels so that they don't find their way into a clump on the floor. Ideally, you'll also be able to incorporate a hamper in your bathroom's layout so that dirty towels go right where they belong, taking the shortest possible journey to get there. Of course, depending on the size of your bathroom, you may be able to store a complete supply of towels on shelves or cabinets or in another storage unit.

Hanging Around: Towel bars are the preferred type of storage for most people. Although you'll select a style based on what suits your tastes—from brushed nickel to stainless steel to chrome to wood—you should be careful to buy towel bars sized to hold the number of towels you need to hang at a given time. You may have to buy more than one bar and stack them, or buy a rack with two or more bars. You can also buy a single unit that incorporates a towel bar underneath a shelf. This gives you the option of storing folded towels above hanging towels and can help you keep a full supply of backup towels handy.

▲ **Basket Bounty** Creative storage can sometimes be the best way to ensure a copious supply of clean towels. This attractive basket adds decorative and portable storage to the bathroom.

▶ **Stacked Odds** This well-appointed bathroom features a wall-mounted chrome unit that boasts a deep shelf for plush folded towels and a hanging bar to keep a towel ready for use. Easy to install, this sleek unit complements the other chrome accents in the room.

The only requirement for towel rack location is that the towels be able to hang unimpeded and not block crucial bathroom fixtures such as a toilet-paper dispenser or radiator. In a crowded bathroom, the back of the door may be the ideal spot for a towel rack. Free wall space is fairly abundant in larger bathrooms, letting you position the rack where it is most handy—preferably where it can be reached from the shower or bath. If your bathroom is large enough and you like your walls just as they are, you can buy a freestanding towel valet that can be positioned wherever convenient. Lastly, if young kids use the bathroom, position towel bars lower than normal.

orderly innovation

If you live in a part of the country that experiences cold winters, you might want to opt for a heated towel rack. It's a European luxury with universal comfort appeal. The racks require an outlet nearby, and most have multi-level bars that require fairly significant wall space. Available in color-coated metal and chrome versions, they can be the ultimate bathtime indulgence.

▲ **Style Pile** On these elegant built-in glass shelves, a collection of towels is kept neat and tidy and right at hand for the bather stepping out of the tub.

Roll or Fold: When it comes to storing your bathroom towels, there is no need to stick with the conventional. If towel bars don't appeal to your design sense, you can choose to store towels folded or, for a less formal look, rolled up. Folded or rolled towels lend themselves to, wider range of storage options than hanging towels do. You can use open shelves for organizing folded towels and box or cubby-type shelving for rolled ones. (Whenever you use shelves for long-term storage of towels, it's best that they be of slotted or mesh construction to allow for airflow and prevent moisture buildup.) Folded towels can also be kept in a large basket, crate, bucket or combination of unusual containers. If you have a separate tub and shower, a ledge over the tub may be an ideal place for folded towels. Wherever you place towels, make sure there is some sort of air circulation around them and that the bathroom is vented to prevent moisture from collecting.

Containment: In addition to storing towels prior to use, you need to provide someplace for towels that are wet and those that need to go to the laundry. If you have long towel bars, wet towels can simply be hung back on the bar unfolded to dry. But if there is not enough room on the bar, or if you have chosen to store clean towels folded or rolled, you'll need an additional place for wet towels.

• **Hooks or pegs** are a simple and effective solution for keeping wet towels off the bathroom floor. These are usually small enough that they don't affect the décor, although you can choose hooks or pegs to match other fixtures in the room. They come in all the finishes in which towel bars and

▲ **Small Wonders** A tiny powder room under a staircase still needs to be organized—a feat that is achieved here with the help of a small antique wrought-iron shelf-and-towel-bar unit. Extra towels and soap are collected in a simple basket on the shelf, and extra toilet paper is attractively jumbled in a larger basket on the floor.

faucets are available. Regardless of what it looks like, a hook or peg needs to be placed where there will be good air circulation, or near a heat source such as a radiator or a heating vent.

- **Laundry bags and hampers** are ideal bathroom additions. Keeping the laundry bag where the towels will be used goes a long way toward preventing dirty towels from becoming floor clutter in the bathroom or bedroom. They can also keep dirty clothing invisible; nothing detracts from the décor of a well-designed bathroom like a pair of underpants or a T-shirt wadded on the floor. If you have the room, a standing laundry hamper with plenty of capacity is the best option. Choose one with a bag liner so that you can just pull the bag out when it comes time to take the load to the laundry room. There's a hamper to match any bathroom's design, whether it's ultra-contemporary, country, or traditional. Just make sure to go with a hamper big enough to hold a week's worth of the family's towels and laundry. Of course, if you have a large bathroom, you can include a big hamper with three compartments, to preseparate the laundry into darks, lights, and whites. But more likely, you'll be squeezed for space. If the bathroom has no room for a standing hamper, use a hanging laundry bag, with eyelets that latch over hooks you attach to a wall or the back of the door. Or choose a laundry bag that hooks over the top of the door. These bags come in range of colors. Inexpensive types are plastic, but burlap or cotton offers a nicer look.

orderly innovation

Some homes don't have a laundry room, and even where there is a separate laundry space there is often too little room for hand-washing and drying delicate garments. With a simple fixture or two, you can equip the bathroom for hang-drying delicates. Install a retractable laundry line on a wall of the shower for quick-access drying space. Look for a "hotel" model—the kind with a chic chrome disc attachment—for a drying line that won't detract from the look of your bathroom. Another option is a retractable drying rack. These are chrome accordion-style devices that fold almost flat against the shower wall when not in use.

storage alternatives

Towel storage and the sink area are rarely enough to contain all that needs to be stored in the bathroom. Additional storage should mesh with the rest of the design elements in the bathroom. For instance, if you've gone for a spare, modern, minimal look, you probably want to use a streamlined cabinet for additional storage rather than a shelf crowded with small containers or a visually complicated étagère. On the other hand, a white pine country bathroom with claw-foot tub cries out for wood shelves with stressed wrought-iron brackets, and lots of decorative apothecary jars for storage of small items. The idea is to adapt available storage options to suit both what you need to store and the look and feel of the bathroom.

Shelving and Mounted Cabinets:

The choice of shelves or cabinets depends on whether you want storage that is concealed or exposed. If you intend to use decorative jars, boxes, canisters, or other containers, select shelves. But if you want a place to put bottles of rubbing alcohol, ointments, suntan lotion, and similar supplies, you should go with a cabinet for appearance sake. Shelves are less of an aesthetic factor than cabinets. Simple glass shelves are the most common, but whatever type you choose, visual appeal is usually dominated by what you put on the shelf. The same is not true of cabinets, which can be focal points that reinforce your design. For instance, a wall-mounted gym locker can be appropriate and fun in a bathroom that boys share while providing lots of concealed storage.

style file

Bathroom cabinets have come a long way since simple medicine chests ruled the day and provided almost all of the concealed storage in the bathroom. Contemporary options include clean white wood cabinets that can be personalized with a bit of paint, elegant frosted-glass units that let you see shapes but still conceal what's inside, and more dramatic steel versions. When looking for a cabinet to add storage to your bathroom, measure both the wall area where you want to position the unit and the maximum number of inches the cabinet can stick out without obstructing free movement in the bathroom.

▲ **Sweet Suite** Even a luxurious bathroom needs to have useful storage. A built-in shelving unit serves the purpose much better than cabinets would, allowing the towels to make a decorative color accent and providing a surface for candles and attractive bottles of personal care products.

▲ **Tub Mate** A tall round basket with lid can be the resting place for a bather's towel, a tray with candles on it, or reading matter for a long, leisurely bath. The basket also doubles as storage for extra towels or as a laundry hamper that keeps used towels and clothes out of view and maintains the spartan look of the bathroom.

149

Storage Units: When you need more storage than you can find under the sink or up on the walls, you should look at independent storage units. The first step in choosing extra storage is to determine how much and what type of storage you actually need. For instance, tall bottles of bath salts or shampoo require significant vertical space. You'll also need to determine whether the storage should be exposed or is better concealed. Once you have a good idea of your storage requirements, match the storage unit to the look of the bathroom.

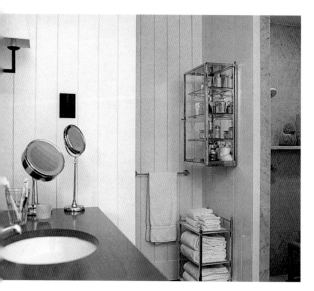

▲ **Sleek Peek** Ideal storage solutions combine fabulous form with no-nonsense function. Here, the owner opted for a clean and elegant glass-and-chrome cabinet for toiletries and personal care products, and a matching shelving unit to keep all the towels in order.

Étagères are freestanding units with legs that straddle the cistern tank, allowing them to fit in even the most cramped bathroom. These are ideal for adding plentiful storage without getting in the way. The scope of available design options means that you can match an étagère to just about any bathroom style. Your choice should be based on the balance of exposed and concealed storage you desire; some étagères are stacked box cabinets, others are sets of shelves, and many are combinations. Where space is not an issue or where you need to store even more than an étagère can handle (or if you don't like the look of an étagère), contemplate other pieces of storage furniture.

Standing cabinets can be fashionable accent pieces in the bathroom. Glass-fronted cabinets are popular for their ability to supply a good deal of storage while complementing many different décor styles. Cabinets without doors can showcase striking bottles of bath products and attractive small storage containers. Special cabinets are made for corners and range from triangular hutch-style pieces to simple chrome pyramids that fit snugly into a corner, out of the way of traffic. If you decide a standing cabinet would best suit your storage needs, be sure to measure the floor space you want to dedicate to the cabinet.

Organizing Accents: Small organizers can accent the look of your bathroom while keeping items such as loose cosmetics in one place. Whether you keep a stack of small decorative hand soaps in an old-fashioned flour jar or use sleek stainless-steel magazine racks to keep bathroom reading materials in order, small accent organizers are the clutter-fighting finishing touches. You'll find scores of jars, trays, and storage boxes in stores, and you can adapt containers from other areas in the house. If what you're storing doesn't need to be hidden from view, use a clear container. For instance, a simple glass jar with cork lid can be used to hold a full supply of cotton swabs. Or use jars, bottles, and boxes without lids. For example, keep an assortment of hairbrushes in a topless stainless-steel canister on a shelf near the sink. Or collect a family's selection of toothbrushes in a small blown-glass vase. Group containers of similar shapes or materials for a pleasing visual composition. Be restrained though: A mixture of too many different types of containers can create a jumbled, chaotic look.

▲ **Double Vision** Twin sinks make for harmony in a bathroom shared by two busy adults. This formal duo keeps things perfectly separated with identical towel bars and shelves for each sink, kept tidy with the help of glass containers.

funtastic
kids' rooms
The Two Meanings of Neat

organized fun

A child's room needs to be one of the most adaptable spaces in the house. It is a playroom that must accommodate toys of all kinds. At a moment's notice, the room becomes an amateur artist's studio, where paints, modeling clay, crayons, and general art supplies are used to express creativity galore. In the next instant it's a clubhouse where your children meet and interact with friends. And, of course, the room has to meet the same needs any other bedroom does, with a place to rest, somewhere to dress, and perhaps a modest reading or study area.

Designed to Change: When a single space has to fill all these rolls, efficient storage and organization become more important than ever—and more of a challenge. But organizing the space shouldn't mean making it look like an adult's room, or creating a bland, generic bedroom. You can create a sense of fun and organize the space so that the décor reflects your child's personality.

As you develop storage and organization solutions, look for options with a decorative flair that can be altered as your child grows. The choices you make should meet your child's needs and style today as well as be able to adapt to his or her ages to come. The best organizational tools serve your child from infant to toddler to preteen to teen. Selections that endure will cost the least in the long run

and look great at all times. It's just a matter of planning for change.

Whichever solutions you choose, you'll face the challenge of maintaining order after they are in place. Many kids don't inherently feel a need to keep their space orderly; they don't mind living amidst disorder. That's why the clutter-beating strategies you use in their

▲ **Pit Stop** A child's miniature car collection is kept orderly with a series of attractive block shelves mounted with hidden hardware. Each car has its own shelf so that the child knows just where each car goes when playtime is over.

rooms will have to be apparent and natural to do and, whenever possible, actually fun. It's a wise idea to include kids on shopping trips for storage, encouraging them to become part of the solution.

The process of organizing a child's room begins with an assessment of what his or her current needs really are. Does your son or daughter have the appropriate space to do homework, play games, and get dressed? What types of clutter are a problem? Creating order in a child's room should be done area by area, incorporating flexible solutions that help your child stay organized even as he or she uses the room for all its many purposes.

orderly layout

For most kids, the bed isn't just a place to sleep. It's a play area where they can rough-house with friends, a make-believe fort, a comfortable space to hang out and much more. That's why the vicinity around a child's bed is so often clogged with toys, books, and other clutter. From baseball caps hung off bedposts to science experiments left on a nightstand, the challenges to keeping this area under control are numerous and diverse. For the purposes of organization, this area includes the bed, under-bed storage, hooks and shelves around the bed, and the nightstand.

The storage in this area should make anything your child needs or uses in and around the bed as handy as possible. There are also long-term storage possibilities in this space that can be stylishly exploited to augment the capacity of closets and dressers.

Bed as Cargo Space: More than just a place to sleep, a child's bed presents abundant storage opportunities. Even a baby's crib has potential: Use fabric bumpers with pockets for soft toys, or buy organizers that hang from the foot or head of the crib and hold diapers and other accessories. The best of these can be removed and used with a stroller.

▲ Ideal Infancy Keeping a newborn's room tidy can be just as challenging as organizing an older child's space. This room is laid out for function and neatness, with a central unit combining crib, shelves, and a dresser.

1 Use Timeless Organizers: It's better to incorporate painted or natural wood chests and shelves and wicker baskets that can be reused than to focus on plastic cartoon-character trunks and bins that will have to be discarded or given away as your child outgrows them.

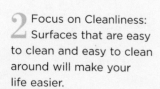

2 Focus on Cleanliness: Surfaces that are easy to clean and easy to clean around will make your life easier.

3 Suit the User: Choose organization aids that are age- and size-appropriate, and place storage where little ones can reach. If you make tidying up their room easy, children are more likely to do it themselves.

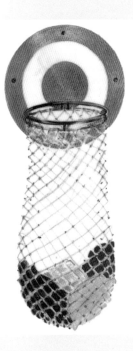

4 Make Storage Fun: When a jumble of toys becomes a collection, and storage methods become a game, kids will help crush clutter without knowing that it's work.

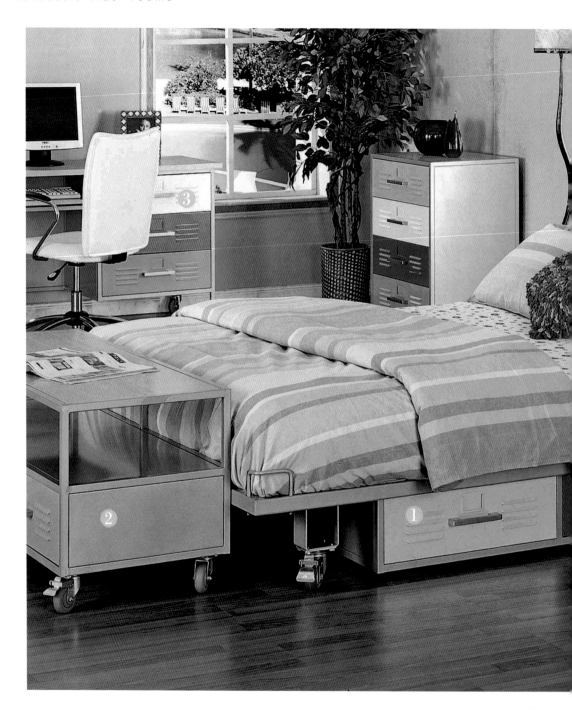

Tidy Teen

This teenage girl's room is a case study in color-coordinated storage options.

1. Exploiting the underbed area, two large drawer units provide a place for long-term and seasonal storage.

2. A rolling unit at the foot of the bed can fulfill many roles. The drawer space can actually replace a dresser, and the top surface can be used as a place to sit when getting dressed or as extra work surface when doing a school project. Equipped with casters, the unit can be easily moved wherever it's needed.

3. A compact desk provides just enough work area for a place to write and a computer monitor and keyboard. The drawer space allows for supplies such as computer disks, notepads, and pens, and pencils.

4. The nightstand serves as a multifaceted storage unit, with a deep drawer for reading material, address book, a journal, and other personal items, and shelves for decorative or functional storage.

UNDERBED STORAGE

Underbed storage units can accent an otherwise plain area. Look for the style that suits your child's room while meeting his or her storage needs.

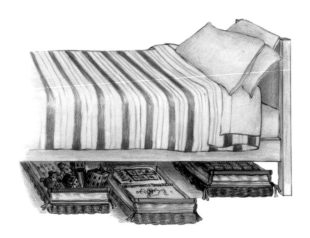

1 You can adapt underbed storage to any child's room. Unfinished metal "locker-style" under-bed drawers bring a distinctive look to a boy's room. Girls might prefer wood-framed boxes trimmed with fabric skirts like these.

2 Brightly colored translucent tinted plastic boxes bring fun and vibrancy to any kid's room.

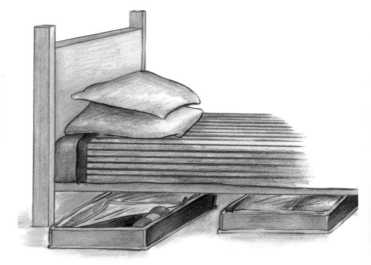

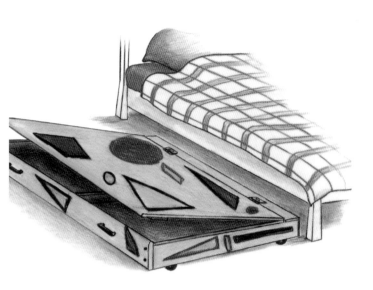

3 Buy unfinished wood boxes or bins and stain or paint them to match the room's décor. You can even work with your child to create personalized designs which, hopefully, will make him or her more likely to use the boxes.

4 Plain steel wire, mesh, or plastic units are an easy solution, and one that can go into other rooms after your child is grown. With these, you simply let what you store make the fashion statement.

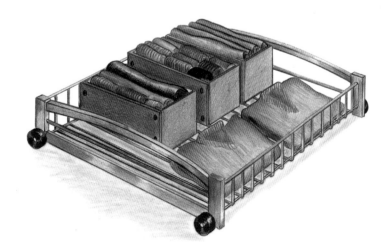

Once your child moves past infancy and into a standard bed, the storage potential increases. The type of bed you select will determine what kinds of storage you can use with it. A simple frame holding a mattress and box spring leaves room underneath that can be taken advantage of with independent underbed storage units. A captain's bed incorporates drawers or cabinets into the bed frame. The head of the bed also presents opportunities; manufacturers make a host of headboard styles with built-in shelves, compartments, and cabinets.

• Independent underbed storage includes bins, boxes, and other containers that slide or roll under the bed. At one time these were limited to plastic units, but today's versions include many stylish options. Choose an enclosed container to store items better left concealed, such as hobby supplies, or those that you want to keep dust free. Boxes with flip lids are often easier for children to use; you may prefer a self-contained unit with frame and a slide-out drawer. Help your child out by picking clear or mesh boxes or bins so that he can see what's stored and find it more easily. Clear containers are also a good choice for attractive items such as colorful sweaters or seasonal bed linens. If what you're storing is less attractive, or you will be the one using it, you can opt for opaque containers in just about any color of the rainbow (and black or white). You can also buy specialized underbed containers for storing specific items such as shoes. To make the storage as easy as possible to use—for both your child and you—select a unit with a handle and wheels.

• Built-in underbed storage most commonly takes the form of ample drawers integrated into the frame of the bed, producing what is traditionally called a captain's bed. These are available in several configurations and can include both pull-out drawers and cabinets with doors. If the drawers are large and plentiful enough, they can actually replace the dresser as primary clothes storage. However, balance the number of drawers against the appropriate height of the bed. For instance, you can purchase a high bed with five or six drawers under it for a maximum of storage space, but a small child may have difficultly getting in and out of bed.

• The headboard is no longer just a nondescript fixture at the top of the bed. These days, headboards for children's beds can include a great deal of small-item storage, from shelves for paperback books to cubbies specifically sized to hold CDs. Headboards with built-in storage can be quite handy for teens, but smaller children may tend to fill the space with a lot of loose items that shouldn't be around the bed in the first place. In addition, this type of headboard takes up more vertical and horizontal room. If you intend to use one for storage in your child's room, make sure to measure carefully before buying.

Nightstands: The size of a child's nightstand should be limited to the space needed to store what really belongs in the area. This is essential because children so frequently put things down without thinking. If your child is a toddler or youngster, look for a nightstand with shelves or a single top surface. Flat, open surfaces allow you to see what is being put there at

a glance, so you can quickly catch the half-eaten candy bar or bug collection before it becomes a problem. Drawers are more challenging, becoming all-too-convenient repositories where many things can be put and forgotten. Drawers in a young child's nightstand too often become cluttered with pieces of gum (chewed or not!), single army men, lonely hair bows, and other items that belong elsewhere. However, you may want to consider a nightstand with drawers if

▼ **Undercover Agent** This two-drawer underbed unit fits perfectly with a teen's room décor, offering a wealth of storage space for extra blankets or seasonal clothes. Low-profile casters allow it be rolled out from below the bed.

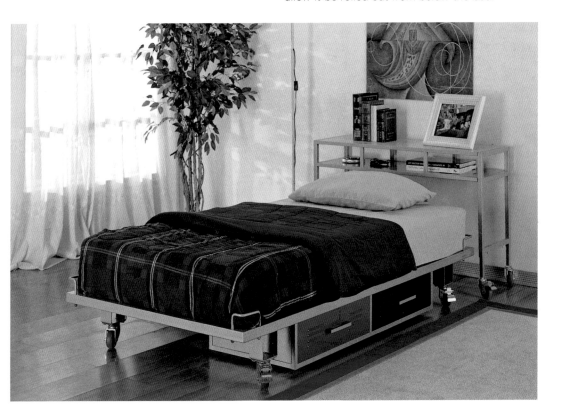

Toddler Time

The storage solutions in this room perfectly suit the young boy who occupies it. All the features have been chosen to help a small child be as independent as possible while learning to keep a small space neat and orderly.

1. High, wall-mounted shelves are used for decorative toys and caps that parent—not child—will select and reach.

2. Open shelving puts favorite books and toys in plain view and within easy reach of the room's occupant.

3. Six big underbed drawers replace a dresser in this youngster's room. The low drawers are easier for the small child to reach, and combining drawers and bed in one unit conserves space.

4. A shelf unit with pull-out wicker baskets is perfect for toys and laundry. The baskets can be removed and taken to wherever the child is playing, and it's obvious to the child where the basket should be put back. The baskets themselves are durable and can withstand rough treatment.

you're the parent of a teen—older children can actually make use of a nightstand drawer or cabinet as a place to keep a journal and address book, an electronic organizer, and books to be read.

Keep in mind that a nightstand is an accent piece in a child's bedroom; there's no reason it has to be anonymous or boring. Choose from many fresh and funky designs in furniture stores or adapt a piece to suit. Repaint a simple stool in vibrant colors to add a fun spark to your young child's bed area. Or repurpose an old metal typewriter stand for an unusual note in the eclectic décor of a teen's bedroom.

Chests, Trunks, and Benches: The
foot of the bed is a great place for a bit of extra storage that doubles as a sitting place for your child when dressing or for friends when they visit. However, don't buy a chest or trunk if you're not sure what would go in it—it's likely to become a hiding place for things that are better discarded or donated. Benches can provide handy seating, but again, limit the surface area to avoid clutter. Slotted bench seats, or other styles with openings in the surface, are good choices because they ensure that small items can't be left on the bench.

▲ **Tough Guy** A rugged steel nightstand can take any abuse a teenage boy can dish out. The deep drawer provides enough space to keep personal items out of view, and the sturdy shelf below can hold a laptop or several schoolbooks for bed-bound study sessions.

▶ **Streamlined Stand** A young child's bed area is clutter-free, thanks in part to a modest nightstand that can hold only a light, a vase, and a favorite toy. Notice that the chair at the foot of the bed uses a large stuffed animal as a placeholder—ensuring clothes don't get piled there.

Complete Bed Systems: Bunk beds and loft beds can be relatively basic sleeping structures, but their construction can also allow for amazing amounts of storage. You'll find loft beds with desks, bookshelves, small closets, and places for computer equipment all contained in the space under the bed. Some bunk beds include complete shelving units with cabinets and drawers. These units can be all-in-one solutions and can even replace dressers, nightstands, and computer desks, but they are also significant investments that may be difficult to find a use for once children have outgrown them. Consequently, bed systems make the most sense in a home where younger siblings are likely to use the unit in later years.

Bedside Shelves: A well-placed shelf can often eliminate the need for a nightstand, supplying all the bedside storage a child will need. If you want to keep bed-area clutter to a minimum and only need room for a light, clock, and the latest book being read, use a single wall-mounted shelf positioned right by the head of the bed where your child can easily reach it. If your son or daughter likes to listen to music or play video games on a handheld game console—or if he or she is old enough to have a wallet and cell phone—you may need more than one shelf. You can even find wall-mounted shelf units with a drawer underneath.

style file

You can spruce up and personalize boxes, storage trunks, chests, wall-mounted cabinets, and other self-contained storage units with decorative treatments that serve to identify what's being stored. Use funky stencils from an art-supply store to label containers. Or to help young children who haven't yet learned to read, clip photos of what's inside to the front of the container or attach small pieces of art from magazines in simple paper frames to show container contents and let children know what goes where.

◀ **Double Time** Sleep and work are sleekly combined in this stylish one-piece desk-and-bed unit. This space-saving piece of furniture can give a school-age child an expansive area for homework and projects, with a fun loft bed just a climb away.

a tidy work and play area

Unless your child's room is sizable, a single area will serve as a place for doing home-work, playing with toys and board games, launching into art projects, and enjoying hobbies. Of course, if you have the space, it's ideal to create different areas for doing homework and working on the computer, creating art, and playing games with friends. But whether this area is spread over several locations or is centralized in one place, the organizational strategies are the same and suggest the furniture you should choose.

The Multipurpose Table: The right worktable provides an ideal place for your kids to have fun and actually helps contain the mess and clutter of different activities. In most cases, the table will be used from the toddler stage until the child is a preteen (once kids reach twelve or thirteen, they tend to focus their activities around a desk and computer setup or in conversation nooks, such as a pillow-strewn floor or bed). Keep this in mind when selecting a table and you should be able to find one that suits your child for nearly a decade of use. The basic choice is between specific-use tables, such as art tables, and more basic general-use tables.

▲ **Custom Playroom** Preschoolers delight in a play area that is rugged enough to withstand a little roughhousing and sized to their stature. This table—with an art-paper roll built in and milk-crate chairs—can tolerate abuse and allows kids to be creative and then easily tidy up.

• **Specific-use tables** are designed for particular activities and combine storage and a work surface in one piece of furniture. These types of tables are useful if you have more than one child or if your child is especially enthusiastic about art projects such as painting, drawing, or working with clay. Although many of these tables are constructed of wood that can be painted or refinished, most are made of materials such as plastic that lend themselves to easy cleanup. The tables can include side shelves, drawers, slide-out bins, rolls of sketch paper on handy bars, and special compartments for small supplies. The more complex the table, the higher the price.

• **General-use tables** come in a range of surface finishes and designs, from natural wood grain to metal. They also come in different shapes, including round, square, and rectangular. One advantage to basic tables is that they can be used elsewhere, for instance as a children's table at a holiday meal. Regardless of style, the ideal table has enough room for your child to spread out. Although these tables are not as task-focused as specific-use models, they can be equipped to enhance neatness with accessories such as a tabletop carousel organizer or pouches that clip onto the edges of the table.

Shelves and Bins: Extra storage units are the all-important supporting players in the room where your child works and plays. The best units can store items of many different sizes and shapes. For instance, a set of bins in a freestanding rack can organize art supplies, keep small pieces of clothing in order, hold toys arranged according to type, or a combination of these functions. Shelves are just as flexible and allow you to display your child's efforts with modeling clay, his or her favorite books, a collection of stuffed animals, and video games.

◄ **See Shells** A teenager keeps a seashell collection on display using simple ledge shelves with hidden mounting brackets. A small desk serves as a homework area, with a desktop carousel and a magnetic wall board to keep important documents and pictures organized.

• **Bin systems** store items right where kids can see them, like shelves and other open storage. But the big advantage with bins is their portability. Some units include many small bins with lips, which are hung in a rack frame. Others are simple wood or metal frames into which the bins slide. Many units feature multicolored plastic or wood bins that allow you to color code what is stored—one more way to ensure kids know where everything goes. You can also create your own bin system—reflecting your own design aesthetic—by using adapted bins, such as boxes or baskets placed on book shelves, a table, or other flat surface. Whichever type you choose, the guiding principle is that your child can remove the bin that contains the items he or she wants, take it to where they'll be used, and easily replace everything when he or she is done. Your choice of bins should be guided by the space you need for what you want to store.

orderly innovation

Art supplies can be instruments of joyful childhood expression. They can also be messy, hard-to-deal-with clutter. You can allow your child creative freedom while keeping the room in order with one of the many complete art kits available in toy stores and art-supply stores. These usually contain a selection of watercolors, colored pencils, chalk, rulers, erasers, and more. The kits come in many different types of boxes, but all are durable and easy to clean, with slots for each item. They let kids take their art supplies to where they'll use them and make it easy to put everything back right where it belongs.

• **Turn to shelves** for open storage to accommodate both similar and disparate items. Place common items such as books, model cars and planes on a shelf so that they can be on display and near at hand. Or use shelves for decorative containers that keep small loose items in check. Freestanding shelves can be quickly moved to wherever you need them, and many varieties—such as stackable shelving units—are expandable to meet your changing storage needs. Wall-mounted shelves have to be placed more carefully because they are harder to relocate, and they are often less stable for small children whose motor skills are not fully developed. But wall-mounted shelves are a good option for teens as media shelving for near the computer or near their beds. Varieties of specialized shelving are available as wall-mounted or freestanding units. These include cubby shelves with slots to hold small items, CD and DVD shelves, and combination shelves with hooks or pegs underneath. Regardless of what type you choose, opt for basic designs that can do duty in other rooms after your child is grown.

Toy Keepers: Every child's room needs a definitive place for loose toys. Any container used for toys should be either expandable or purchased to accommodate the current volume of toys and about half again as many. Your child's age is going to affect what type of storage you use. Dealing with infant toys is an issue of portability because toys must accompany the baby everywhere to keep him or her entertained. That's why folding or collapsible toy bins are best for an infant's room. Inexpensive, durable, and easy to clean, these are usually made of synthetic-fiber mesh with pliable frames.

For toddlers, standard toy chests are a traditional and effective way to keep ever-growing toy collections under control. These capture a full assortment of toys in one place. The simplest are wood boxes with lids (and childproof hinges so that your child doesn't pinch his or her fingers) that can function as toy chest, bench, and—after the child has grown—long-term storage for blankets or other items.

But general toy storage need not be limited to the conventional. Manufacturers offer a panorama of choices from the innovative to the wacky. Choose based on the types of toys you need to store and on your child's personality. A little girl's bountiful stuffed animal collection can be placed on a shelf or in a toy chest or bin but will enliven the room and increase your daughter's enjoyment if grouped together in a hanging toy "hammock." Corral ball collections in an oversized fabric laundry bag. Keep action figures together in decorative tin bins lined up on a shelf. Whatever general toy storage system you choose, make sure it can be put to another use and can be made to fit with the decorative style of other rooms, because your child will eventually outgrow it.

style file

Make your child's toy collections a decorative element to keep them stored efficiently. For instance, a traffic jam of toy cars can be displayed in a row on a narrow shelf. This will keep them organized and create an interesting and age-appropriate accent for the room. And your child is likely to enjoy the display so much that he or she will remember to return the cars to their rightful place when playtime is finished.

A Desk for All Seasons: School-age children benefit from a dedicated workspace where they can tackle homework assignments and school projects, and where they can keep and work on a computer. Although you can use an existing desk or buy a basic adult model, keep in mind that the better suited the desk is to your child's work habits and needs, the more productive he or she will be.

A carefully chosen desk will not only meet your child's current needs but still be useful in years to come. Many children's desks offer adjustable legs and other contemporary features such as computer monitor stands, keyboard trays, built-in cord channels, and bookshelves. Purchase the right desk and it may well serve your child into his or her college years.

▲ **Toy Holes** A child's play area stays chaos-free via a wall of built-in cubbyhole shelving. The toys can be rearranged periodically to move currently popular items to lower, easy-to-reach shelves.

the closet and dresser

Clothes clutter is never a simple thing to design out of a home, and this is nowhere more true than in a child's room. Children tend to leave clothes wherever the clothes come off, and they often have trouble with the idea of a hamper, much less keeping their closet organized. The way to establish order among your child's clothes and to train your child to maintain organization in the closet and dresser is to make clothes placement as obvious and intuitive as possible. Both the closet and the dresser can be used exclusively for clothes or adapted for other types of storage, and both should change over time as your child grows. It's also important to understand that as children age, the differences between boys and girls become more pronounced. The teen girl is likely to want a closet and dresser that reflect her tastes as well as her clothing storage needs. The teen boy is more likely to need efficient functionality to prevent the entire bedroom from becoming a clothes-strewn mess.

Canny Closets: The first rule of setting up a closet in a child's room is that the mix of storage—hanging, flat shelf, bins, drawers— will have to change fairly regularly as your child grows. Whatever configuration you use, it should be user-friendly if you hope to keep the closet organized. For instance, placing clothes

on a shelf out of the reach of a small child makes independent dressing nearly impossible and almost ensures that garments will wind up scattered on the closet floor. Fortunately, you can pick from many options in setting up a child's closet. You can make the most of an existing closet by incorporating organizers that

▲ **Convertible Furnishing** Planning ahead will pay off in this little girl's room, where the solid-wood changing table converts to a dresser when potty training is completed. The piece can be refinished to suit just about any décor as the child grows.

suit your child's needs. If the bedroom will ultimately be used by several brothers and sisters, and you're willing to invest more time and money, you may want to build in the features to accommodate your children. But often, the most efficient, comprehensive, and economical solution will be an all-in-one closet organizing system.

• Comprehensive closet systems can be a simple, one-stop-shopping solution for the busy parent. You can choose from among numerous all-in-one closet systems on the market. Most retailers offer design and installation services in addition to selling the hardware and accessories. These systems are extremely adaptable in design, allowing you to configure the closet to precisely meet your child's needs and move elements such as hanging bars, shelves, and drawer units around as you prefer. Manufacturers also offer many accessories, such as bins, belt racks, hanging organizers, and more. You can choose from a variety of finishes, ranging from simple coated wire units with steel brackets to solid wood or veneered pieces with hidden attachments that create the look of an entirely built-in unit.

• Individual organizers are an excellent way to create exactly the storage your child needs. By mixing and matching organizers and storage units, you can quickly and easily make a closet age-appropriate and adaptable. This gives you maximum flexibility when the time comes to change things around. And it offers a way to accent your child's closet with small decorative touches that complement the design of the room without making major structural changes or undertaking large cosmetic projects. Hanging units are some of the handiest organizers for a child's closet. You can use overdoor fabric or plastic units with pouches for toys, shoes, or other small items. A simple column of fabric shelves hung from a closet pole will help organize your child's clothes by days of the week or keep sports gear organized by event. Make use of existing shelf space by employing bins, trays, or boxes as homes for socks, underwear, headbands, and other loose garments. A plastic or metal footwear rack with slots for individual pairs of shoes will go far in alleviating the jumble of shoes that slow your child down when it comes time to dress.

• Built-in closet elements require more work to install, but, depending on how complex the configuration is and the materials you use, a built-in design may actually be cheaper than a prefabricated closet system. This option also gives you a chance to create exactly the look you want, from painted or stained wood to steel or melamine.

Kids' Closet Storage:
A Changing Equation

Children's closet storage needs change over time. Different life stages call for different types of organization if the closet and bedroom are to remain clutter free.

- **Infants:** A nursery closet need only be useful to you, because the room's occupant certainly isn't going to be using it. Filling the closet with shelves is the best strategy in a baby's room because there's no need to hang an infant's garments. If you need a space for loose supplies such as wipes and lotion, use small boxes or bins on the shelves.

- **Toddlers:** Small children require a minimum of hanging space because most of what they wear can easily be folded. In addition, this is the stage at which children begin to learn to dress themselves, and toddlers have a hard time handling hangers. To make it clear where things go in the closet, use exposed storage such as shelves wherever possible. If you incorporate bins or drawers, pick translucent or transparent units so that the child can see what's inside. Use illustrations or photographs as labels to help the child easily find what he or she needs to get dressed.

- **Young Children and Preteens:** Simplicity is the essential factor in a successful preteen closet. Children don't always focus on dressing, so closet solutions need to be intuitive and easy to use. Hooks, slide-out shelves, and shoe cubbies will work best for this age group. Drawers will be less effective because they are likely to become cluttered with loose items that are quickly shoved in and then forgotten.

- **Teens:** A teenager's closet should be similar to any adult's, with minor differences. The teenage boy requires less hanging storage than a teen girl, who is more likely to wear garments that crease if folded. Teens can be trained to keep the closet neat if you cluster similar garments together—jeans in one area, sweaters in another—and provide plentiful space for their clothes. Use overflow storage in a dresser or shelving unit as necessary.

Teen Scene

This organized teen's closet is far more appropriate for the user than the traditional and out-of-date long-hanging-bar-and-one-shelf combination.

■ A minimum of hanging storage—but enough for short and long garments—provides all the hanger space a teen boy will need.

■ Shoe cubbies not only supply plenty of space for the footwear collection, there's enough room left over to store other small items.

■ Well-spaced shelves provide so much usable storage area that they don't seem overburdened, and everything on them is kept neat. There is enough space left over to display models and other toys.

■ Combined with the various other types of storage in this closet, the wall-mounted drawer unit provides the space needed for underclothes and other folded items, eliminating the need for a dresser.

■ A catchall basket keeps loose items contained and in sight. Without some sort of organizer, these things would wind up cluttering dresser tops and bedroom floors.

Dresser: Folded clothes small and large find a commonsense home in a child's dresser. Assigning portions of each drawer—or an entire drawer—to one type of clothing is essential to making the best use of this space. This strategy not only ensures that children know where to find underwear, shirts, shorts, and other garments, it also goes a long way toward preventing them from loading up the dresser with toys and other loose items they want to hide away. Dividers can be used to section off dresser drawers so that when children rummage around for a shirt or socks they don't mess up the whole drawer. Made of wire mesh

style file

Dresser styles are limited only by the boundaries of your design sense. You can find a slew of themed dressers that look like racing pit crew toolboxes or are decorated with flowers and other designs that will appeal to kids. But the simpler the dresser the more likely you'll be able to use it through different stages of a child's life, and to different design schemes in the house once your kids are older.

or wood, these partitions are available at home centers and large retailers.

The dresser offers another, often overlooked, storage area—the top surface. Assign this surface a storage function, such as holding a row of books or a collection of stuffed animals, and you head off the practice of "dumping" objects on the top of the dresser. The top surface is also a good place for bedroom essentials such as a lamp or a fan. Younger children can make do with a plain dresser, but older kids will probably prefer a dresser paired with a mirror. This may function as an organization device itself, because older children concerned with how they look will take pains to avoid blocking the mirror with clutter.

▼ **Two for One** This bed not only does double duty as a comfortable couch—with its four posts and twin headboard and footboard—it is also neutral enough to complement any bedroom in the house once the teens in this room move out.

▼ **Seeing Double** Dual dressers add the storage space that is lacking in the cramped bedroom closet that two preteen daughters share. Cube-style wall-mounted shelves are ideal for a teen—nothing falls off the end of the shelf. The shapes accommodate books and CDs as well as the keepsakes a teen girl naturally wants in her room.

supplemental storage

If your child's room includes entertainment electronics, you'll need to institute storage solutions that keep electronics from cluttering the space. The room may include a stereo, TV, DVD player or VCR, computer, video game console, and all the bits and pieces that go along with them, and they all need to be kept organized. The easiest way to do this is to use one piece of furniture to contain all electronics. In the case of stereos, you can purchase wall-mounted or freestanding stereo racks with room for components, speakers, and CDs.

▶ **Changing Times** This changing table takes up a small area, but the storage potential is maximized. The table's shelves are organized with rows of wicker baskets containing diapers, towels, and dirty laundry. Two wall-mounted shelves are fitted with rails, making them ideal for securely showcasing baby's books and stuffed animals.

Storing individual media such as CDs, DVDs, tapes, and video games with the electronics they'll be used in goes a long way toward heading off clutter problems. You'll find a huge selection of TV stands and racks that incorporate shelves or cabinets for different peripheral devices, with room included for DVDs, video games, and other extras. For a kid's room, it's best to buy a rack or stand with casters so that it can be easily moved for cleaning or when the room needs to be changed around.

orderly innovation

Keeping toys and other loose articles in check offers a chance to add decorative compositions to your child's room. Use three or four galvanized steel buckets or smaller steel painter's pails to hold a collection of building blocks, toy cars, or action figures. Leave the buckets unfinished for a cool look—hanging from pegs or lined up in a row along the floor. Or spray-paint the buckets in high-gloss shades to create custom color accents. You can do the same with wood buckets of all sizes or use inexpensive plastic beach pails. Buckets of any type are a great style enhancement and they make handy toy containers that are extremely portable.

▶ **Locker Room** When a child's closet is just too small to contain everything that needs to go there, look for a wardrobe or other piece that can hold favorite clothes. This gym-locker-style cabinet contains a rod for hanging clothes and deep shelves for sporting gear, folded clothes, or other items that need a place to go.

living areas

Organized Relaxation and Entertainment

the gathering place

Living rooms and family rooms are convertible spaces with specific areas designated for different activities. Some spots are ideal hideaways to enjoy solitude, reading, or just relaxing. Other areas of the same space may serve as cozy nooks or conversation pits conducive to intimate entertaining with close friends. No doubt, you have a space dedicated to enjoying TV or a movie, and the same locale serves as a comfortable zone for family members to relax and unwind together playing a game. These areas may also be called upon to blend into one general space for hosting large events and parties when the need arises.

Simplicity Style: The different zones and roles of your living areas can actually span more than one room. Many homes have both a casual family room and a more formal living room.

But the organizational strategies for these rooms bridge any spatial separation between them. Whether you have separate family and living rooms or one big room that serves all your entertaining and relaxing purposes, the tactics you'll apply to keep order and maintain the flow of style through the house are the same. The basic design principle in common living areas is to define and separate areas within the room by function, and to make the furniture work as hard as it can at keeping different areas free of clutter and looking as chic as possible.

After you divide the room into functional areas, the organizing and choosing storage options becomes much easier. You can make choices depending on what activities are common in any given area, and, ultimately, you make the areas more comfortable, attractive, and enjoyable to use.

▶ **All Around** A simple tray-top coffee table holds a few books, leaving room for an occasional teacup or wineglass. The unusual end tables serve their own purposes: the trunk on the right holds seasonal linens, and the table on the left is kept more than an arm's reach from the sofa, ensuring it won't be used for anything but decorative display.

1 Be Area Aware: Organize different areas differently to suit the activities specific to the area.

2 Shelf It: Shelves are storage chameleons that can change to suit your needs. Versatile and available in diverse styles, shelving units can be the answer to a host of family-room clutter quandaries—they also add visual interest to the décor.

3 Contain, Contain, Contain. Small bowls and containers are your friends. The more loose items you have on surfaces, the more will gather there. Dedicate bowls, bins, and boxes to the loose items of life, like keys, coins, and pens.

the conversation area

Every living room should have one: an area for social interaction, usually defined by a sofa, easy chair, or loveseat (or a combination), with a coffee table as centerpiece. Often there are side tables and more formal chairs, but the idea is always to make a comfortable area that invites socializing. This is usually the first place people will gravitate toward upon entering the living room, and it can be used in many ways, from a quiet spot for a busy couple to discuss the day's events over a drink to a cozy locale to entertain family and neighbors.

▶ **Cozy Chunk** A modest coffee table provides just enough room for a vase full of flowers and a light snack, serving this bright and intimate conversation area well. Although the top surface of the table is wisely limited, the base is solid and chunky, giving the table enough visual weight to keep it in scale with the rest of the furniture.

▼ **Double Time** Small ottomans or upholstered tables can be great alternatives to a single coffee table. They can be easily moved to put snack or drink trays in front of people or rearranged to suit the design of the room. The bright canary yellow used here adds a splash of color to an otherwise basic living room.

The main fixtures in the area include seating, such as sofas and overstuffed chairs, and tables, such as a coffee table and end tables. Not all of these will be part of your living room layout—they may be dispersed between living room and family room. Couches and chairs generally don't need much organization, although it helps to keep throw pillows to a minimum to keep remote controls, magazines, and small items from disappearing. Although end tables may play a role, the center of any conversation area—and the spot where the biggest clutter challenges lie—is the coffee table.

Coffee Table: This essential piece of furniture provides a handy place to set down drinks and snacks, a location for magazines and catalogs yet to be read, and a home for decorative centerpieces that provide focal accents. Of course the table itself is a decorative element, one that comes in literally dozens of variations. But apart from the table's style, the more critical decisions concern size and storage capacity.

◀ **Pillow Talk** This plush sectional sofa works with a solid coffee table to create a wonderful social center in the corner of an urban living room. The coffee table design includes no lower shelf that might become crowded with reading matter and bric-a-brac, and the top surface is largely taken up by a decorative serving tray, a vase of flowers, and a square of candles.

COUCH PARTNERS

Coffee table designs seem to know no bounds. Getting away from the traditional wood rectangle, with or without drawers and shelves, opens a whole new world of possibilities.

Glass-Top Single-surface glass-top coffee tables are a perennial favorite for their ability to resist stains in a busy living room, and for their style, which is suited to a range of décors. This type of table also limits what can be stored, because there are usually no extra shelves. Find glass tables in square, rectangular and round shapes.

Kidney-Shaped

Kidney-shaped coffee tables have a retro but enduring look that fits in with many living rooms. These too are usually offered without lower shelves or drawers, minimizing the amount of irrelevant stuff that can be put on the table.

Cubes Cubes have caught on as options to a single coffee table. These small boxes come in different materials, but most are constructed with lids and hollow interiors for hidden storage. Cube tables give you the freedom to create a useful composition in the space a traditional coffee table would occupy: use three in a row, two side-by-side, or create a square using four cubes clustered together. Available in metal, dark and light wood, and even upholstered versions, there's a cube for just about any décor.

Bench-Style Bench-style coffee tables add a modern flair. Some form a solid, upside down U, while others are more stylized, with slotted tops and solid legs. These are great choices for minimizing surface area and providing a clean, streamlined look.

▲ **Light Holder** An end table should have a specific reason for being or it is better left out of the room design. The end table on the left is used to hold a lamp, with no extra shelves or drawers that might serve as collecting places for clutter.

Size of Coffee Table: The first thing to consider is the actual size of the piece; it should match the scale of other furnishings in the room. This is not only a matter of style; coffee table size will affect the practical aspects of using the piece. A coffee table that is too small will not provide adequate surface area for transient items such as beverages and food when you are entertaining. And one that is too large will get in the way and invite clutter.

This is not to say that an existing coffee table won't serve your purposes. You can adapt the furniture you own. For instance, a bottom shelf on a coffee table is prone to sport old newspapers, odd dishes, and other clutter. But rather than buy a coffee table without a bottom shelf, you can clutterproof your existing piece by filling the shelf with decorative boxes used to store coasters, pens and notepads, and other small items. This is a great way to create an attractive composition, add small storage to the room, and defeat disorder all in one stroke.

The same principle can apply to the top of a coffee table. Perhaps the surface seems to attract loose mail, cell phones and many other items that don't belong. Create a simple composition of three vases to take up the majority of the surface, leaving enough room for a couple of beverages or a magazine. Family members will be less likely to put down random items where there's no room for them.

All this assumes you use a traditional coffee table with legs. But your options are certainly more extensive than that. For a unique look, turn to unconventional pieces, many of which offer a wealth of hidden storage. Chests and boxes make for visually and physically solid coffee tables. They also contain enough interior space for seasonal linens or extra slipcovers for the sofa and loveseat. Along the same lines, you can create an eclectic look by using antique luggage or stacks of oversized books as your coffee table.

End Tables or Not: The choice to include end tables in your living room layout should be based on need. End tables can be useful as a place to position a lamp, keep a phone handy, or showcase a blown-glass bowl or vase. But they can also become drop zones for all manner of odds and ends if they are merely included as a natural part of a living room suite. If you opt to include end tables, the rule of thumb is the simpler the better—no drawers unless you have something you want to keep in them, and no extra shelves unless they, too, will be used for specific storage.

the entertainment center

The contemporary explosion of consumer electronics, digital and high-definition TVs, and movie and programming options has meant that entertainment gear and accessories play an increasingly important role in our living areas. More and more, family or living rooms are equipped with complete entertainment centers that provide an audio and video experience on par with small movie theaters.

▼ **Tune Room** The shelves behind this living room conversation area have been dedicated to housing audio components. The stereo tuner, turntable, CD player, and speakers have been given their own spaces along the bottom of the shelves. Custom shelves above the electronics contain a CD collection.

▲ **Flat Out** This exceptional bookcase has been fitted with a central panel that serves as a mounting surface for a state-of-the-art flat-panel TV. Other audio and video components have been placed in the cabinet on the lower right of the bookcase. Cables are hidden and run behind the bookcase.

The downside of high-tech involves the over-abundance of cords, components, peripheral devices, and add-ons that must be effectively organized if they are not to become an unattractive mess. Proper positioning and the correct housing for all your gear will determine the quality of the viewing and listening experience, as well as how streamlined your entertainment system will appear.

Tech Talk: Begin by planning for the components. What will you include? Do you have both a DVD player and VCR? Do you have a collection of DVDs and videos, or do you mostly rent them? Will you connect the TV to your sound system to create a home theater or do you want audio and video systems kept separate? Are you going to include a video game console? If so, how many controllers and how many games do you anticipate having in your collection? Do you have a CD "jukebox" or will you need storage for your music? Setting up home entertainment systems that are easy to use and offer maximum enjoyment is a matter of thoughtful planning.

When you've determined what technology you want to incorporate, you'll need to decide on where and how you'll house the various components. That means choosing furniture that will provide a comfortable location for all your equipment and media and at the same time add something to the look of the room.

orderly innovation

Using a remote control with your electronic components does not necessarily mean those components have to be out in the open in a direct line of fire with the remote. If you prefer concealing electronics such as stereo equipment behind a panel or cabinet door, you can buy small discrete signal boosters or pickups that will allow you to use a remote even when a door or panel is covering the equipment.

Adapted Units: You may already have a large wardrobe, standing chest, or other piece of furniture you want to adapt for use as an entertainment center. The challenge is to match the existing piece with the physical dimensions of all your gear. Often this means augmenting whatever piece of furniture you are using with other media storage, such as special racks for DVDs or CDs, or a separate stereo cabinet. You also may have to modify the piece of furniture you have chosen so that it has the right number of shelves and compartments for everything you need to store, and so that cables can run freely throughout. When considering an existing unit for use as an entertainment center, carefully assess whether the unit really provides the space you need for components, cabling and other necessities. It's always better to go bigger and have extra storage space.

Building in Your Entertainment: Although expensive, a built-in entertainment center will ensure all your electronics have the space they need and neatly fit exactly where you want them, in relation to each other and to the furniture in the room. This is also a way to seamlessly integrate home electronics into home design, so that they seem an integral part of the décor. If planned correctly, built-in units can house speakers, audio components, a TV, and all other elements of the system without any exposed wires and cables. When creating a built-in unit, it's a good idea to use flexible features wherever possible, including slide-out shelves on rollers, cable access panels, multiple speaker hookups in case you want to change the acoustics of the system, and doors and panels that can be removed when it comes time to update the décor. Built-in or not, you must have access to the back of your electronics, not only for hooking up different elements but in the event you experience problems with a given component or decide at any time to upgrade equipment.

Building custom housing for your home audio and video equipment also gives you the chance to personalize the style of the unit to suit your tastes and décor. For instance, if you have a sleek modern house and furnishings,

▲ **Integrated Entertainment** A built-in entertainment center allows a homeowner to position electronics exactly where he or she wants them, without disrupting the flow of the room's design. This electronics alcove includes a custom space for a large-screen TV, a shelf for home theater components, and custom drawers along the side to hold DVDs and CDs.

you may choose to leave the fronts of your components exposed for a high-tech look. In a more traditional setting, you might opt for cabinets with dark wood, raised panel doors, and silver or brass speaker screens concealing the speakers themselves. You can also incorporate storage features that meet your specific needs, such as a drawer with dividers to keep your extensive DVD collection in order.

▼ **Scene Setting** A media center cabinet easily contains a home theater system, with stereo components and a TV. The TV is viewable from any seat in the horseshoe arrangement of furniture, a setup that is also conducive to socializing when the TV is off.

Prefab Entertainment Centers: The selection of available entertainment centers includes one for almost any décor and electronic setup. If your needs are not complex, consider a basic television stand to hold just the fundamental video pieces such as cable receiver, DVD, VCR, and your TV. Stands come in many different finishes, including metal and wood of all colors and stains, and styles from high-tech to retro. However, if your equipment is more extensive, you'll want to look at entertainment centers with larger capacities, perhaps even full-blown wall-size units that can house a fully outfitted home theater setup.

All-inclusive entertainment centers take up a lot of room, so you'll need ample available floor and wall space. The advantage to these large structures is that they are designed for ease of use. Easy-access cable cavities are built in, so that hooking up your equipment is a very straightforward task. You can also select units with amenities such as large drawers with special dividers for CDs, DVDs, videos or video games. You can even buy a unit that includes a special cabinet for a video game system, or other extras such as additional shelving for general storage.

The styles of these units are as diverse as living room décor schemes, but aesthetics must come second to function in choosing a complete entertainment unit. First and foremost, the main compartment should roughly match the size or your TV: too small and the TV won't fit, too big and the TV will look lost and silly in position. The center must also house all the components you want to keep with the TV. Electronics come in many different sizes, so it's a good idea to measure yours before you select an entertainment center. The unit will also need to accommodate speakers unless you've decided to use separate stands or mounts for your speakers.

▼ **House Speaker** A partition divides the conversation area from the entertainment lounge in this stylish living room, but the stereo can play throughout the space courtesy of futuristic stand-alone speakers—sleek enough to fit right into the décor of the room. The speaker cords have been run through the partition, keeping the wires and connections hidden and the space neat.

The Separate Stereo: You may want to put your stereo and TV in different areas. It may be that you don't have room for all the components combined, or perhaps you don't intend on using the stereo with your TV and want to physically separate them. In some cases, stereo acoustics will be better in a different location. Whatever the reason, you'll find plenty of storage solutions specifically made for stereo systems.

• **Minisystems or shelf stereos** are small stereos that combine separate components in one portable unit. This type of stereo can be placed on a shelf or can be positioned on minisystem stands made to hold them. The stands are usually metal, with an unadorned base and a single shelf for the stereo. You can also buy matching speaker stands. Some versions are freestanding; others are wall mounted.

• **Component stereos** are usually organized in their own racks or cabinets. There are two basic types of stereo furniture for component systems: enclosed and display. If you like the look of your stereo and it fits in with the rest of your decorative elements, pick a rack that doesn't conceal the components. Exposed storage also makes it easier to set up and use the equipment. Choose between a modern look with a high-tech post-and-platform construction, or

▲ **Metal Jacket** The entertainment is kept out of sight in this contemporary living room, hidden behind sliding metal panels. Notice that the compartment has been fitted with shelves for the components and special shelves for cassettes, CDs, and DVDs.

▶ **Pole Vault** Tension-pole shelving systems are sleek and adaptable, and can be customized with components that meet your precise storage needs. This system in a modern living room keeps books and pictures organized and offers hidden storage in a row of attractive drawer units.

more traditional box cabinets that contain adjustable shelves for the different parts of a stereo system. You can easily find a style of cabinet that fits in with existing living room furniture. The basic "box" style comes with different wood veneers and surface finishes. Or you can opt for more stylized stereo cabinets, with touches such as legs and raised panels that make the cabinet look like a more traditional piece of furniture.

• **Speakers** often call for their own supports. Leaving speakers on the floor can deaden the sound and may cause the thump of the bass to travel to other rooms in the house. Pick from several different types of speaker mounts and stands. If you prefer to keep the floor clear, buy speaker slings—simple hammocks that are hung from the

ceiling. Or choose more solid mounts that bolt into the wall or ceiling and allow you point the speaker wherever you want the sound to go. Freestanding speaker stands are available short and tall, in metal, wood, or plastic, and in natural finishes or colors. Make your selection based on your personal style and the size and weight of your speakers.

orderly innovation

Modern modular shelf systems are some of the most visually dynamic pieces of living room furniture available, not to mention their tremendous storage capacity. These include tension-pole systems in which the shelving is held by sleek adjustable poles positioned between floor and ceiling. You can also opt for a high-tech bracket system, in which floating brackets are affixed to a wall and serve as the base for stylish shelves. Both of these types of systems are sold with a variety of components, from drawers fronted in brushed steel to colored Plexiglas bins. If you're drawn to a contemporary aesthetic in home design, these systems offer as much style as storage to any room they inhabit.

Bookshelves not only add storage to your home, they can also be key architectural, structural and decorative elements.

1 Use bookcases to camouflage walls that are in bad shape or bring balance to oddly placed window and door openings.

2 Custom shelves bring function and visual interest to bare, out-of-the-way areas, such as under a staircase, below a window seat, or in a seldom-used closet with the door removed.

3 Use open bookcases as dividers to visually and physically split up a long, narrow room, while still allowing light to flow through the space.

4 Add visual height and symmetry by building bookshelves around a door or window.

the versatile shelf

Shelves provide some of the most efficient and useful storage you can use in living areas. Shelf space is ideal for organizing anything in plain view, from a row of books to magazines in library cases to a collection of favorite vases. But shelves can also support concealed storage in the form of containers, such as boxes, bins, bowls, and slide-out drawers. The decorative advantage to shelves is that they are reasonably innocuous; they fit right into any décor. Which isn't to say shelves can't make a dramatic style statement—a single ebony-colored wall-mounted shelf set against a neutral wall can make as strong a focal point as anything you could put on it. Available in light, dark, and unfinished woods, and metals from brushed nickel to bright and shiny chrome, shelves can provide just the accent look you seek. Although there are two basic types of shelving—mounted and free-standing—the sizes and variations within each type let you match shelf to storage purpose quite neatly.

Mounted Shelves Small and Large:

Wall-mounted shelves let you put storage at exactly the height and location that works best for you. The fundamental difference between the various mounted shelves available is the method of mounting. Traditional mounted shelves use brackets; some are adjustable, but most are not. Brackets range from the purely functional to artistic versions that are essentially architectural ornamentation. Inexpensive shelves often sit on steel arms supported in a slotted track that is screwed to the wall. More chic brackets range from antique wrought-iron standards screwed to the underside of wood shelves to ornate plaster corbels across which a stone shelf is placed.

Increasingly, homeowners are turning to the cleaner look of hidden mounting hardware. Hidden or "keyhole" brackets provide invisible mounting so that the shelves seem to float on the wall. This gives you the chance to create a composition on the wall, such as staggering a trio of floating shelves. It's also a way to put a single shelf exactly where you want it, one that looks nice but doesn't call attention to itself. Hidden mounting is also used with more specialized shelves, such as cubes—square shelves that hang solo or in groups and completely surround whatever is stored in them.

orderly innovation

Create a two-sided wall of shelves by placing tall, sturdy case bookshelves back to back. Not only does this create a great deal of storage space, it can be a solid barrier between two different living room areas. Secure the units by screwing the backs together.

▲ **Book Look** Built-in bookshelves are useful additions to any home, and add distinction to this elegant room. Not only do the shelves keep a leather-bound collection in order, the look of the books adds warmth to the room.

- **Built-in shelves** take the mounted principle one step further, integrating a shelving unit with the structure of the room. They are often crafted to include architectural detailing to match molding and baseboards. Your goal is to make the shelving appear as if it were part of the original house construction.

Freestanding Shelves: You'll find a multiplicity of types, styles, and designs on even the most modest shopping trip for independent, stand-alone shelving. The choices among closed-back, traditional standing units are supplemented by a profusion of more unusual manifestations. "Ladder" bookshelves have no back. They are constructed with side posts and shelves, and made to lean against a wall, providing increasingly shallower shelves toward the top of the unit. These are ideal for the conventional hierarchy of book display: smaller paperbacks at the top, and oversized hardcover coffee table volumes at the bottom. It's a unique look that is not for every house. Although they are not as stable as standard case shelves, ladder shelves can be a wonderfully stylish addition to the right living area.

Open shelves—sturdy stand-alone types with no backing—work well against a wall but are especially effective as room or area dividers. This can be very useful in a living room with several different areas that aren't necessarily separated by a wall. For instance, a tall open-shelving unit can break up a long, narrow living room and establish the division between the entertainment area and a cozy reading corner. A long, low unit can separate the living room from a dining area. Wheeled versions offer portability and make changing the living room layout a snap, such as when you need more room for a party.

style file

Bookshelves can hold many things other than books. A solid mass of books on a bookshelf can create a fairly dull appearance. Create more visual interest by breaking up long rows of books with a decorative vessel or statue. Or stack a column of books on their sides as a bookend. If you're storing books you've already read and probably won't be referring to again, consider placing a work of art in front of them.

▶ **Wall Full** The right shelving system suits the space and your needs. This prefabricated unit neatly fits along a living room wall, blending so well that it looks built-in. The unit is completely adaptable, with adjustable shelves, stylish sliding etched-glass panels, and a simple ladder for reaching objects placed on the top shelves.

a quiet reading and reflection area

As much as a living room is a place for socializing and entertaining, it should also offer a refuge, a place where people in the family can enjoy a measure of solitude and pursue quiet activities such as reading a book or writing cards or a letter. Although you can always curl up on a couch, sometimes it's nice to have a small nook you can call your own. A comfortable reading area can be modest in scope, with nothing more than an extremely comfortable chair, a good reading light, and a small side table to hold a book or beverage. The only potential clutter culprit in that trio is the table. As with couch end tables, a reading table should be small and simple. There's no need for drawers unless you require writing utensils, in which case the drawer should be small. Keep in mind that the table needs to accommodate only a lamp, a book and a beverage—no more.

▶ **Couch Cove** This small sofa is nestled in an alcove created by surrounding bookshelves. A small pullout lamp provides a personal reading light for time spent curled up with a favorite book.

▶ **Corner Store** A sun-drenched corner of a living room makes for a perfect reading area day or night. The small table is only large enough for a vase and a few favorite books. A chair and sturdy reading light make this an ideal location for an escape with a good book.

around the fireplace

No other architectural element can match the literal and figurative warmth a fireplace brings to a living room. But, unfortunately, the hearth (the base in front of the fireplace) and the mantel over it present enticing places for people to put odds and ends as they pass through the room. The best way to keep the area free of items that don't belong there is to keep what does belong there front and center. On one side should be a wood carrier or wood crib stocked with a modest amount of wood. Place

▼ **Fadeaway Fireplace** A mantel-less fireplace façade offers a clean and spare surface, attractive and with no place for clutter to accumulate. The hearth is kept free of everything except a useful standing lamp. The owner has kept the room streamlined, with minimal decoration.

a set of fireplace tools on the other side. Cover the front with a fireplace screen, and you have effectively blocked anyone from setting down anything else on the hearth.

Art of Design: The mantel is a slightly different story. Mantels are like spacious shelves—they beg to be filled in. The two main strategies to prevent anyone from doing so haphazardly are to block the mantel with art and to create compositions on it with objects. A large piece of art over the fireplace draws the eye and there is a natural inclination to view it full length. When an extraneous item is set in front, it's jarring to the eye and immediately apparent that the object is out of place.

Compositions of vases, ceramic sculptures, or other decorations take up spare space on the mantel and ensure that loose items such as books find no home there. Use the mantel as a showcase for vessels or other items that you want to display. Change the display at your whim, but remember the goal is to discourage clutter.

▶ **Old Flame** Fireplaces call out for simplicity, and this fundamental living room arrangement delivers. The hearth is furnished with only two andirons, so that anything else positioned there will seem out of place. The mantel is elegantly decorated with a few precious pieces; clutter would seem jarring and be immediately apparent against this composition.

entryways
Arranging Small,
Essential Rooms

a welcoming space

Entryways come in all shapes and sizes, from the self-contained mudroom to the wide-open formal foyer and the narrow entry hall. And, of course, many homes have more than one, with a formal front entryway for greeting guests and visitors and an informal side entrance that is regularly used by family and close friends. But every entryway shares the same organizational challenges. In the bustle of coming indoors, visitors and family alike are likely to discard outerwear and whatever they have brought in with them wherever they can find a place. Keeping these spaces tidy and welcoming means finding a place for all the things that inevitably will be left—whether they belong there or not. This is why storage solutions must account for what is naturally kept there, such as coats, mittens, and other garments, and what is awaiting removal to another area, such as mail, packages, catalogs, and more.

Small Spaces, Big Decisions This exercise in organization is made more challenging by the fact that many entryways are very small. There's a limited amount of space to work with, so storage solutions must themselves be very efficient. They must also be chosen with an eye toward style, because any organizing accessories in this area inevitably become decorative accents. Whether in the front or back of the house, modest or grand, a well-organized entryway makes a favorable first impression on a visitor and a comfortable transition space to the living areas of your home.

▶ Passage Way The simplest entry halls, such as this one, provide a place to temporarily set packages down, some seating to pull off foul-weather gear, and a mirror to check the way you look before leaving the house.

1 Make Room for Clothes: The entryway is where jackets, hats, and other garments come off. Give every garment a place to go and you'll reduce clutter significantly.

2 Be Space Conscious: The storage solutions you use must suit your needs and fit the limited space available.

the entryway closet

Not every entryway has a closet, but where one exists it should be designed to be as useful as possible given the traffic through the door. The three basic elements that any entryway closet should have are a modicum of shelf space for packages, with storage bins and baskets included as necessary; a hanging rod for coats and other garments; and hooks for clothing that does not require a hanger, such as scarves. If the closet is large enough, you can place a rack for footwear inside so that shoes and boots do not mar the look of the entryway. Generally, the most efficient organization for entryway closets is to group garments by season, unless your seasonal outerwear is stored in the attic, bedroom, or elsewhere.

▲ **Hall-Mark Piece** An antique table holds small decorative items in a small entry hall/transition space. There's no room to set down keys or gloves, so clutter is kept to a minimum.

orderly innovation

Making the most of an entryway closet means optimizing all available storage space. Hang a plastic or fabric organizer with pockets on the back of the closet door, and use it for mittens, caps, and other soft, seasonal items that are so easily misplaced.

controlling clothes

As with so many other rooms in the house, the chief source of clutter in the entryway is clothing. Any storage in the area must naturally accommodate different bits and pieces, and must be expandable enough to serve at holidays or family parties when the number of coats, hats, and accessories greatly increases. Even entryways that have closets can use additional hanging devices. Extra clothes storage in the entryway takes two forms: structures that are built in, such as wall-mounted cubbies, cabinets, and hooks, and movable organization aids such as coat racks.

Coat Racks: Space-efficient racks come in both ornate and simple designs. They provide useful storage for jackets and other garments that can be hung and can be placed wherever is most convenient. Even when not in use they look good and can be kept out of the way. Whatever style you pick, the rack itself needs to have a sturdy base to prevent tipping when loaded with coats, and it's wise to buy one with a built-in umbrella stand to take full advantage of the rack's storage potential. Choose from various metal finishes and light and dark wood types.

Footwear Storage: Shoes, boots, garden clogs, and other footwear can be some of the most unsightly clutter in an entryway. Fortunately, it's also one of the easiest things to organize. Use one of the many footwear racks available, buying one that suits the number of shoes and boots you'll need to store in the busiest of times. Some racks have a tray bottom to capture dirt that falls from the bottom of shoes and boots; others are simply bars or mesh or plastic-grid shelves that hold the footwear off the floor. If you use an open-design shoe rack, place some sort of tray or mat underneath to capture water and dirt. For foul-weather footgear that tends to track in a lot of mud, snow, and dirt, use a boot box dedicated to containing the mess. A sturdy plastic or metal bin or box is ideal, because it can be regularly hosed out for quick cleaning. Keep odors to a minimum with cedar foot racks. These are especially useful in the close confines of a closet, which should smell every bit as good as it looks.

▶ Hunting Day This almost whimsical entryway features abundant decorative character with antlers that double as hat racks and a line of riding boots that stand alone as decorative accents. A brass umbrella rack and a unique piece of furniture meant for canes and hats round out the entryway storage.

If most of the footwear that will be stored in the entryway is clean, you can use cubby-style shelves that will keep everything organized in visually appealing storage. Cubbies are especially handy in homes with small children, who can be taught to remove shoes before coming into the house proper. You can label the storage spaces with their names or pictures of their shoes.

Hanging with Hooks and Pegs: Individual hooks and pegs can quickly be positioned right where people take off coats and scarves. But more often than not, hooks or pegs will be integrated into a larger, more complete unit, such as a wall-mounted shelf or wood rack with a row of pegs or hooks below. These generally present an informal look, but you can find hooks in a wide range of styles, from unadorned wood versions to ornate chrome pieces that serve almost as architectural detailing.

mail, keys, and other small items

With clutter it's often the small things that matter, and in the entryway they tend to defy endeavors at neatness. That's why you need to turn to dedicated storage units to help keep little things from becoming big frustrations. In almost every entryway, this means finding a place for mail, packages, and keys. You may also need a place for cell phones, personal music devices, and other electronics that are used only outside the house.

orderly innovation

In larger entryways with no closet, a wardrobe can supply stylish extra storage space. Available in many different wood finishes, these pieces of furniture offer an abundance of storage, including a hanging rod, drawers, shelves, and often places for footwear. Or sometimes you can incorporate these in a wardrobe that lacks them.

Specialty Organizers: Choose from a full selection of storage units designed just for mail, keys and other small items, available from large retailers and catalog suppliers. These include wall-mounted mail sorters with slots for standard-size envelopes and larger catalogs; key hooks or peg sets; and combination units with shelves, mail slots, coat pegs, and key hooks. Although the majority of these are simple wood units, some are crafted of metal in various finishes. Buy one to suit your décor or, if you have a

Welcome Respite
A simple but smartly furnished entryway serves family members and visitors alike.

1 Long coats and seasonal garments are stowed away in the hall closet.

2 A wall-mounted unit incorporates pegs for hanging casual coats and scarves and a top shelf for gloves or folded items such as the blanket shown.

3 Mail is kept in check by an oversized tray, which can be moved to an office or living room where the mail can be perused whenever convenient for the homeowner.

4 An antique trunk adds flair and foul-weather-gear storage to the space. It can also be a place to sit down and remove footwear.

5 A decorative basket provides an appealing holder for umbrellas.

formal, visually spare entryway, keep a key and mail organizer concealed in a closet or a cabinet.

Decorative Storage: You can save the expense and limited decorative options of store-bought small storage aids by putting existing decorative bowls, tins, boxes, and bins into service in the entryway. Use a set of ceramic bowls for pocket change, keys, and other loose items such as lipsticks. Or keep small items contained in a pretty bamboo bin or small stone box. You can hold mail in almost any shallow, broad container, from a lacquered serving tray to a large, hammered silver platter. As long as the container can reasonably fit what you regularly need to store in the entryway, let your imagination and design sense be your guides in adapting storage.

furnishing for transition

Any entryway benefits from a place to sit for a moment, whether to just gather yourself after bustling in the door or, more likely, to take off shoes and jackets. In a formal vestibule, this may be a nice chair or settee. More often, it will be a slightly more utilitarian piece of furniture that can stand up to use by children and busy adults, something more akin to a well-appointed bench than a Chippendale chair. In the best of all possible worlds, this piece of furniture will serve more than one function, offering a place to sit and some sort of storage.

Hall Trees: These are traditional entryway pieces, ranging from refined Queen Anne designs to simple oak country versions. Regardless of style, the basic design is the same: a small square seat is backed with a tall mirror or paneled back, which is often topped with a shelf or cabinet. The mirror can be a wonderful addition to the entryway, letting people check their appearances before stepping out or right after they take off their coats when arriving. The seat is usually meant for one person, and often has storage in a box under it. Sometimes, shoe shelves are built into the space under the seat.

▶ Bench Bounty Making the most of a closet-less entry required installing a hall tree that not only provides sufficient seating for visitors, but also affords abundant hidden storage under the lid. A shelf displays objects d'art and hanging pegs hold hats and jackets.

▲ **Entry Consolation** This entry is given a formal look with a console and mirror. The console serves merely as a place for lamps and to set down packages and mail that are brought into the house. It's limited size means clutter can't easily accumulate.

THE BEAUTY OF BASKETS

Baskets can be just the multipurpose catchall an entryway needs. Given the diversity of designs available, baskets can accent the formal foyer just as easily as they fit into the rough-and-ready mudroom. It's simply a matter of picking the baskets that best serve your storage needs in a material that accents the room.

1 Small, fairly flat tray baskets make ideal small-item valets.

2 Shallow steel-mesh or wire baskets provide a place for mittens, gloves, and scarves, with air circulation available to promote drying and prevent musty odors.

3 Deep baskets can be ideal for boots or large packages waiting to be mailed.

Benches: Perhaps the most versatile seating for an entryway is a bench. This allows several people to sit down at once, offers a solid base for wrestling with boots and galoshes, and allows for different types of storage underneath or on the sides. Bench units come in all sizes and shapes, from an elementary designer style like a slat bench to solid units with a flip lid and a box underneath to benches with compartment towers on one or both sides. Storage underneath can be very valuable, especially if you want to keep seasonal clothes for children and items such as dog leashes out of view but handy. If you prefer to use baskets for storing garments such as gloves and caps, consider an open storage tower. If your needs are more basic—just a place to pull off boots and shoes and somewhere to leave them—consider a basic boot bench with a shelf underneath for shoes and boots.

orderly innovation

Every family member brings things into the entryway and needs, at one time or another, to remember to take things along when leaving. Whether it's mail and school backpacks coming in or lunches and packages going out, everything should have a place of its own. If yours is a busy household with adults and children coming and going, incorporate visually pleasing organizers in the form of in/out containers. Depending on how many things each family member regularly moves in and out of the entryway, the containers can be small wicker baskets or larger tin boxes or decorative bins. Create a uniform look by using containers of a single type for every family member, or go with a more eclectic style by using different containers for each person.

General Storage: Occasionally, the entryway is large and busy enough to support a separate storage structure. Although shelving units can provide accessible storage, they are usually out of place in a well-appointed front entryway. More often than not, the best choice for additional entryway storage will be a freestanding cabinet or low side table. These provide hidden storage for the myriad items that might usually overwhelm the space if stored out in the open, as well as a flat top surface that can be used for decorative storage containers. A mirror placed over one of these pieces gives the arrangement polish and integrates the piece into the space.

index

index

index

index

photo credits

Gordon Beal • page 63

Tim Beddow • pages 6 (bottom left),
    21, 36, 119, 225

Timothy Bell • page 198

Fernando Bengochea • page 167

Eric Boman • pages 60, 110

Antoine Bootz • page 149

Courtesy of California Closets • pages 29, 31, 80, 178

Courtesy of The Container Store, 800-786-7315,
    www.containerstore.com • page 170

John Coolidge • page 50

Paul Costello • pages 22, 28

Anthony Cotsifas • page 2

Grey Crawford • pages 117, 128, 133

Susie Cushner • page 85

Roger Davies • pages 95, 114 (bottom)

Jacques Dirand • pages 114 (top), 120

Carlos Domenech • pages 142, 201

Pieter Estersohn • page 32

Carlos Emilio • pages 145, 191, 209, 223

Dana Gallagher • pages 58, 69, 144,
    212 (bottom), 216

Oberto Gili • pages 15, 53, 99, 192, 219

Tria Giovan • pages 5, 107, 121, 124, 125, 150, 190

David Glomb and Julius Shulman • pages 6
    (left 2nd down), 59

Courtesy of Grange Furniture, Inc., 1.800.GRANGE.1,
    www.grange.fr • pages 74, 111, 202

Kari Haavisto • page 33

Alex Hemer • page 34

Robert Hiemstra • page 213

Lizzie Himmel • page 154

Image Studios • pages 140, 148

Courtesy of JC Penney • pages 155, 175

Jon Jensen • page 91

Erik Kvalsvik • page 215

Courtesy Ligne Roset • pages 9, 205, 211

David Duncan Livingston • pages 88, 89

Fred Lyon • pages 164, 181

Peter Margonelli • pages 73, 76, 204

Nedjelko Matura • page 61

Maura McEvoy • page 141

Jeff McNamara • page 82

Michael O'Brian • pages 24, 228

Victoria Pearson • pages 65, 122, 126, 139, 143

Santi Caleca • page 44

David Phelps • page 94

Daniel Piassick • pages 152, 180 (left and right)

Courtesy of Plain & Fancy Custom Cabinetry •
    page 56

Courtesy of Powell Furniture, Inc. • pages 158, 163, 166
    168, 183, 227

Laura Resen • page 84

Lisa Romerein • page 50

Eric Roth • pages 12, 104, 171, 184, 199

Jeremy Samuelson • page 54

Copyright Snadiero • page 57

Hugh Stewart • page 115

Tim Street-Porter • pages 6 (left 3rd down), 10,
    44, 123, 129

Buff Strickland • page 87

Luca Trovato • pages 66, 151

Simon Upton • pages 212, 221

Dominque Vorillon • pages 6 (right)

William Waldron • pages 1, 6 (left top), 16, 39, 81, 132,
    187

Michael Weschler • page 93

Paul Whicheloe • page 90

Vincente Wolf • page 40

Courtesy of Wood-Mode Fine Custom Cabinetry,
    877 635-7500, www.wood-mode.com • pages
    42, 48, 50

Nigel Young • page 174

Firooz Zahedi • pages 196, 203